Two Months with Mary

SHORT REFLECTIONS

FOR EVERY DAY OF MAY AND OCTOBER

By

Rev. Joseph A. Viano, S. S. P.

ALBA · HOUSE NEW · YORK

IMPRIMI POTEST:

Rev. Edmund Lane, S.S.P.
    Censor Delegatus
    Society of St. Paul

IMPRIMATUR:

+ The Most Reverend James W. Malone
    Bishop of Youngstown

NIHIL OBSTAT:

Reverend James A. Clarke, Chancellor
    Censor

    April 15, 1983

ACKNOWLEDGEMENTS

The Rosary; Papal Teachings. — Selected and Arranged by the Benedictine Monks of Solesmes. St. Paul Editions (Daughters of St. Paul), Boston.

Meditations on the Breviary. By Bishop Angrisani. Vol. IV. Benziger Brothers, New York.

The Image of Mary. By Horacio Bojorge, S.J. Alba House, New York.

Mary, Mother of Christ and of Christians. By Joseph-Marie Perrin, P.P. Alba House, New York.

Illustrations: By Sr. Angelica Ballan, of the Pious Disciples of the Divine Master, Rome.

Cover: by Richard Skerl.

CONTENTS

OCTOBER

FOREWORD

Devotion to Mary is as old as the Church itself. Her whole life, from the time we meet her in the pages of Sacred Scripture when the angel told her that she was to become the Mother of the Son of God, through the birth and boyhood of Jesus, the beginning of His public life at the marriage feast of Cana, His passion and death on Calvary, His resurrection and ascension into heaven, and the descent of His Holy Spirit upon her and the disciples at Pentecost, has been a source of inspiration to countless millions.

The pages of this little book recall the main events in the life of our Blessed Mother and the impact that her example and intercession have had on the life of men and women down through the ages. Each page is a mini-meditation on one or another aspect of our devotion to Mary, ideal for sermon preparation or private reflection.

The thoughts for each day of the Month of May concentrate on the truths we all hold dear regarding Mary as the Mother of God and the mother of us all. The thoughts for October honor her as the Queen of the Most Holy Rosary and include reflections on the mysteries of this still popular devotion.

It is hoped that the sentiments expressed here will lead the reader to a deeper appreciation of the role of Mary in our lives and to a greater love for Jesus, her Divine Son.

Rev. Edmund Lane, S.S.P.

M A Y

DEDICATED TO MARY, MOTHER of GOD and OUR MOTHER

1: May   PRESENTING MARY, THE QUEEN OF MAY

"All graces pass from God to Jesus, from Jesus to Mary, and from Mary to us." — St. Bernardine of Siena.

* * *

To know, love and serve God; to make Christ, Our Redeemer, the Mediator of all graces and the Center of our spiritual life; to recognize the action of the Holy Spirit in the sanctification of our own souls, are all basic and essential truths of our Christian faith. To be devoted to Mary, the Mother of God and our Mother, is also very important in our spiritual life. Mary will help us to get closer to God; she will prepare us to receive all the graces we need from Jesus and the gifts of the Holy Spirit. The Blessed Virgin will make the work of our sanctification and of our salvation easier.

Vatican Council II, in the Document *Lumen Gentium* (Chapter VIII: the Blessed Virgin Mary) declared: "The faithful must reverence the memory of the glorious ever Virgin Mary, Mother of God and of Our Lord Jesus Christ . . . The Catholic Church, taught by the Holy Spirit, honors her with filial affection and devotion as a most beloved mother . . . The Blessed Virgin is also intimately united to the Church . . . and she is rightly honored by a special cult in the Church . . ."

But does Mary really care for us? Undoubtedly. She cared for Jesus, she cared for Joseph, her devoted spouse, she cared for the Apostles, she cared for all the new members of the rising Church, and she cares for each and every one of us, her children, entrusted to her by her firstborn child, Jesus, just before dying on the Cross.

When Bernadette Soubirous was asked: "At the Grotto of Lourdes, did Our Lady look only at you?" "No," she replied, "She looked at all the people, and with great affection; at times she seemed to look at them one by one, and her glance would rest on one or another as if she had recognized a friend."

If Mary cares so much for us, we must, for our own spiritual benefit, care for her too. We must love her tenderly because she is our sweet mother; we must imitate her in the practice of our Christian life, in the acquisition of virtues and in doing good; we must be devoted to her, by praying to her, and we must, with faith, believe in her powerful intercession with God.

* * *

"To love Mary ardently is a sign of lively faith and a certain pledge of salvation." — Pelbarto di Temesvar.

2: May BEHOLD YOUR MOTHER! BEHOLD YOUR SON!

"Whoever does not have a great love for the Mother of God cannot have great love for her Son." — St. Joseph Cafasso.

* * *

The cross was raised. The Blessed Mother, firm, and motionless, remained at the feet of her crucified Son and assisted Him during His long agony, without a sign of weakness or discouragement.

Darkness began to extend a dense veil over all nature. The frightened birds flew screeching to their nests and a sense of terror pervaded the onlookers. Little by little Calvary was deserted; only soldiers on duty, some priests, who still continued to insult Jesus, and a group of pious women remained. Magdalene and St. John were near Mary at the foot of the cross and shared the agony of her heart.

Jesus was crucified between two thieves. What a humiliation for His mother to see Him treated the same as Dismas and Germas! And yet she, as Refuge of Sinners, was already praying for them.

Just as at the wedding of Cana, through the prayers of His mother, Jesus had changed the water into wine, so again now, through her intercession, he transformed a sinner, Dismas, into a saint.

Those three hours were hours of painful agony for Jesus without alleviation of any kind.

All at once the voice of the dying Jesus broke the somber silence of Calvary: "Father, forgive them, for they do not know what they are doing" (Lk. 23:34); and in that hour so sorrowful and solemn, that voice, so familiar to Mary, pierced her heart as a sword.

Jesus was praying for His crucifiers, and His mother, echoing His prayers, prayed for the sinners of all times.

Seven times Mary heard that dear voice, but when, for the third time, Jesus broke the silence it was to make His will of love: "Woman, behold your son;" then He said to John, His beloved disciple, "Behold your mother" (Jn. 19:27).

Mary's mission had been proclaimed: she was to be our mother, as we were to be her children.

In reality, that will was Jesus' leave-taking of Mary. She knew it, but in her thirst for souls, similar to that which burned in Jesus' heart, she accepted with love the duty of becoming the mother of the human race. Mary has watched over us ever since. If we could only understand what an object of solicitude we have been and are to our heavenly Mother!

* * *

"O Lord, I thank You for having created the Blessed Virgin Mother, for having made her so beautiful and for having given her to us as our Mother." — St. Leonard of Port Maurice.

10

MARY, MOTHER OF GOD
MOTHER OF THE CHURCH, AND OUR MOTHER

"Mother of God! What an ineffable title! The grace of the divine maternity is the key which opens up to weak, human scrutiny the untold riches of Mary's soul: as it is likewise a challenge commanding for her the utmost reverence of every creature. — Pius XII.

* * *

Mary is the Mother of God, as the Council of Ephesus defined in 431. Can we understand the wealth of meaning contained in these three simple words: Mother of God? Can God unite Himself more intimately to a creature than through the mystery of motherhood? What an exceptional place in God's love must be held by the woman whom He chose from all eternity, to form the body of His Son, to nourish Him, to educate Him until He reach adulthood. When one thinks of God's infinity and of the nature of His activity, which is love, how can one measure the love with which God has encircled His Mother from all eternity?

Mary is the Mother of the Church. At the end of the third session of Vatican II, Pope Paul VI solemnly proclaimed Mary "Mother of the Church." When we call Mary Mother of the Church we re-emphasize the fact that she belongs to the Church, just as any mother is truly a part of her family where she always holds a place of special honor. Mary, according to Pope Paul VI "is the greatest, most perfect, most important and most chosen member of the Church." Mary is truly the mother of each member of the Church, whether clergy or laity. When we contemplate the Church, we also find Mary. Paul VI also said: "Knowledge of what is, in fact, true Catholic doctrine on Mary will always constitute a key to our true understanding of the mystery of Christ and the Church. Mary, therefore, in so far as she is the Mother of Christ, is also the Mother of all clergy and faithful, that is to say, of the whole Church."

Mary is our Mother. She is the greatest, the loveliest, the most powerful mother. The words of Jesus on the cross, "Behold your Mother," which summarize all that Mary should be to us, are capable of changing an entire life. De Montfort said: "He has not God for his Father, who has not Mary for his Mother." And St. Bernard: "The reason for our love of Mary is the Lord Jesus; the measure of our love for her is to love her without measure."

* * *

"Mary alone by her dignity transcends heaven and earth . . . She is at once the Handmaid and Mother of God, a Virgin and yet a Mother." — St. John Chrysostom.

11

4: May   MARY, THE GREATEST WOMAN OF THE BIBLE

"A great sign appeared in heaven: a woman clothed with the sun, and the moon was under her feet, and upon her head a crown of twelve stars." — Apoc. 12:1.

* * *

In Genesis, Mary, the new Eve, is simply described as the WOMAN who will crush the serpent's head, and bring a new life into the world, through the redemptive power of her offspring. Isaiah said that "A virgin will conceive and bring forth a son, the Redeemer." All the prophets talk about the promise of a great woman who will bring salvation to the world by giving birth to a Savior. Holy writers of the Church compared the virtues of this woman to the virtues and deeds of great women of the Old Testament: Sara, Lia, Rebecca, Judith, Ruth, Queen Esther . . . .

Finally, in complete obscurity, this Woman was born, exempt from original sin, and her name was MARY. She lived a quiet life, she gave birth to Jesus, the Redeemer, but she is mentioned only three times during His public life. She spoke very little, and out of 27 books which make up the canon of the New Testament, only four mention Mary by name, while one speaks of her only as the *Mother of Jesus* or *His Mother* but *never mentions* her by name. The four books are the Gospel of Matthew, Mark, John and Luke with the Acts of the Apostles. St. Paul in the Letter of the Galatians mentions Jesus "born of a woman."

It is clear that the Evangelists speak of Mary with the ultimate intention of saying what they desire about Jesus. Their discourses on Christ find light and support in her. Mary is not the Gospel. There is no Gospel of Mary. But without Mary, neither is there any Gospel. So she is not missing from any of the four. She is not only needed for wrapping Jesus in swaddling clothes . . . She is not only necessary for teaching Him to take His first steps, toddling in our world of men. Her mission is not only co-extensive with that of the earthly Jesus, but goes far beyond His death on the Cross; she is present at His resurrection and the rise of His Church.

Garbed with the sun, crowned with stars, standing on the moon, Mary, like her Son, remains forever. The world and the stars will pass, but Mary will go on forever, like the Word of God of which she is the Echo. Mary, the Mother of Jesus, belongs to the store of goods common to Jesus and His disciples. His Father is our Father. His hour is our hour, His glory, our glory. His Mother our Mother.

* * *

"The things promised her by the Lord shall be accomplished." — Lk. 1:45.

5: May   MARY AND THE SECOND VATICAN COUNCIL

"The Council presents our Lady to us not as an isolated figure, but as a most marvelous, beautiful and holy creature, precisely because of the divine mysteries which surround her, giving meaning to her existence, bathing her in light . . . . Mary is distinguished by her high office and her great dignity of Mother of God made man, and is, therefore, the dearly beloved daughter of the Father and the temple of the Holy Spirit. Through this gift of grace she far excels in dignity all other creatures, those terrestrial and those celestial." — Pope Paul VI, 1967.

* * *

Rev. Valentino Del Mazza, SDB, in his book *Our Lady Among Us* said: "Vatican Council II (1962-1965) gave the most authentic and dynamic presentation of Catholic devotion to Mary. Never before did the Christian people have such a rich and fruitful treatise on Mary as we enjoy today in the entire chapter 8 of *Lumen Gentium.*"

I agree with Fr. Del Mazza one hundred percent. Allow me now to present some excerpts from this chapter 8 entitled: *The Blessed Virgin Mary, Mother of God, in the Mystery of Christ and the Church*:

"Mary is hailed as a pre-eminent and singular member of the Church, and as its type and excellent exemplar in faith and charity. The Catholic Church taught by the Holy Spirit, honors her with filial affection and piety as a most beloved mother . . . .

"Mary, consenting to the Divine Word, became the mother of Jesus, the one and only Mediator . . . . She devoted herself totally . . . to the person and work of her Son, under Him and with Him, by the grace of almighty God, serving the mystery of redemption . . . .

"The Blessed Virgin . . . persevered in her union with her Son unto the cross . . . lovingly consenting to the immolation of the Victim which she herself had brought forth. Finally, she was given by the same Christ Jesus, dying on the cross, as a mother to His disciple, with the words: 'Woman, behold your son'. . . . By her maternal charity, she cares for the brethren of her Son, who still journey on earth . . . .

"This most Holy Synod . . . admonishes all the sons of the Church that the cult, especially the liturgical cult, of the Blessed Virgin be generously fostered, and the practices and exercises of piety . . . be religiously observed."

* * *

"Mary is not only our Mother and Queen; she is our sister and companion. She too was a citizen of this world, she trod our streets, and felt more keenly than others do the heavy weight of the vast human family, stricken with so much hurt." — Pope Paul VI.

13

6: May MARY, MODEL OF THE CHRISTIAN FAMILY

"Mary knew the joys and sorrows of the family; she knew also the happy and the sad events, the fatigue of daily work, the discomforts and sadness of poverty, separation's rending of heart. But she also tasted the ineffable joys of family life . . . . The Virgin's merciful heart sympathizes with family needs . . . The divine Mother is a most perfect model of the domestic virtues which must adorn the Christian married state. In Mary you will find the purest and the most faithful love for her most chaste spouse. Her love was made up of sacrifices and of delicate attentions. In Mary you will find entire and continuous dedication to needs of family and home; you will find humility, patient resignation, lovableness and charity to all who visit the humble home of Nazareth." — Pope Pius XII in *Quandoquidem,* April 20, 1939.

* * *

The Bishops of the U.S.A. issued on November 21, 1973, a Pastoral Letter entitled: *Behold Your Mother, a Woman of Faith.* In presenting this very important document the Bishops declared: "We hope and pray that our presentation will be a subject for serious study and loving reflection. We desire with all our hearts that it be received into homes, rectories and seminaries, into schools and institutes of higher learning, into adult education groups, confraternity centers, campus ministries and religious communities." I like to quote, from this Letter, a few thoughts about Mary and Family Life:

"What does Mary mean to today's family? Mother of the Holy Family at Nazareth, Mary is mother and queen of every Christian family . . . God called Mary and Joseph to sublimate the consummation of their married love in exclusive dedication to the Holy Child, conceived not by a human father but by the Holy Spirit.

"Because she is seen as the Mother of all the living, Mary is viewed properly as the guardian of the child in the womb, as well as the child that enters this earth alive . . . . Abortion is a heinous crime and a serious sin.

"Mary is Queen of the home. As a woman of faith, she inspires all mothers to transmit the Christian faith to their children.

"Family prayer, in whatever form it takes — meal prayers, night prayers, the family rosary, attending Mass together — provides opportunities for prayer to the Blessed Virgin."

* * *

"Mary, the most perfect of all mothers, is an admirable example to them of every virtue . . . . Praying for the sanctity of mothers means to pray for a perfect society." — Pope Pius XII.

14

7: May   THE BEAUTY AND POWER OF MARY

"In His own Mother's countenance God has gathered together all the splendors of His divine artistry. Mary's glance! Mary's smile! Mary's sweetness! The majesty of Mary, Queen of heaven and of earth! As the moon shines resplendent in the dark heavens, so is Mary's beauty set apart from all other beauties, which are but shadows beside her. Mary is the most beautiful of all God's creatures." — Pius XII.

* * *

Sculptors, artists, architects, poets, and the most varied geniuses have competed to present pleasing and worthy homages to Mary.

If you think of art, beauty, and love you must think of Mary!

The Liturgy of the Church does not tire of calling Mary: *More beautiful than the moon, more resplendent than the sun, stronger than an army set in battle array.*

Dante Alighieri, one of the world's greatest poets, wrote the most beautiful poem in honor of Mary:

Maiden and Mother, daughter of thine own Son,
   Beyond all creatures lowly and lifted high,
   Of the Eternal Design the corner-stone!
Thou art she who did man's substance glorify
   So that its own Maker did not eschew
   Even to be made of its mortality.
Within thy womb the Love was kindled new
   By generation of whose warmth supreme
   This flower to bloom in peace eternal grew.
Here thou to us art the full noonday beam
   Of love revealed: below, to mortal sight,
   Hope, that for ever springs in living stream.
Lady, thou art so great and hast such might
   That who so crave grace, nor to thee repair,
   Their longing even without wing seeketh flight.
Thy charity doth not only him up-bear
   Who prays, but in thy bounty's large excess
   Thou oftentimes dost even forerun the prayer.
In thee is pity, in thee tenderness,
   In thee magnificence, in thee the sum
   Of all that in creation most can bless.

* * *

"Enraptured in the splendor of your heavenly beauty and impelled by the anxieties of the world, we cast ourselves into your arms, O Immaculate sweet Mother of Jesus and our Mother, Mary . . . . Receive, O most sweet Mother, our supplications, and above all obtain for us that, one day, happy with you, we may repeat before your throne that hymn which today is sung on earth around your altar: You are all beautiful O Mary! You are the glory, you are the joy, you are the honor of our people! Amen." — Prayer of Pius XII for the Marian Year, 1953.

15

8: May   THEY ALL PRAISE THEIR MOTHER AND QUEEN

"The praise of Mary is an inexhaustible fount, the more it is enlarged the fuller it gets, and the more you fill it, so much the more it is enlarged." — Abbot Francone.

* * *

Fathers and doctors of the Church, well known Apostolic Writers, Saints, Popes, scholars, founders of Religious Orders and Congregations, great poets and famous Mariologists down to the last one, Pope Paul VI, through their writings and documents, have only the greatest words of praise for Mary, the Virgin Mother of God and our Mother, the Queen of heaven and earth, the co-redemptrix. Let me quote two of these writers:

St. Cyril of Alexandria, who died in 444, wrote:

We salute you, O Mother of God, greatest treasure of the universe, lamp of inextinguishable light, crown of virgins, indestructible temple, throne of the invisible One . . .

After the fall caused by Eve, the outcast is readmitted to heaven by means of you, O Ave!

Through you baptism is given to believers.

Through you churches are founded throughout the world.

Through you entire peoples are led to penance.

Through you the only begotten Son of God became a shining light to those who lay in darkness and in the shadow of night.

Through you the prophets utter their prophecies.

Through you the Apostles announced salvation to all the countries of the world.

Through you the dead come to life . . . And all this through the will of the Holy Trinity.

St. Bonaventure (1217-1274) wrote this beautiful *Marian Te Deum:*

We praise you, O Mother of God, we proclaim you Virgin and Mother!

The entire world venerates you as Spouse of the Eternal Father!

And to you all Angels, Archangels, Cherubims and Seraphims sing unceasingly:

Holy, Holy, Holy is the Mother of God, Mary ever Virgin!

Heaven and earth are filled with the majesty of your Son!

You are honored as Queen by the whole heavenly court!

You are invoked and praised as Mother of God by the entire world and by the holy Church.

You are the gate of Heaven, the ladder to the kingdom of Heaven and blessed glory!

You are Spouse and Mother of the eternal King, the temple and sanctuary of the Holy Spirit; the altar of the Blessed Trinity.

You are the Mediatrix between Jesus Christ and men, the Advocate of the poor!

You are, after Jesus, our only hope, Mistress of the world, Queen of Heaven!

We bow to you and salute you each day, O Mother of love!

Sweet and good Mary, in you we place all our hope, defend us for all eternity! Amen.

* * *

"If all the tongues of men were put together, they will not suffice to praise Mary as much as she deserves." — St. Augustine.

16

9: May   LOOK AT THE STAR... INVOKE MARY!

"And the Virgin's name was Mary. Let us stop to contemplate this name, which we are told signifies Star of the Sea and which fits the Virgin Mary so perfectly. Nothing is more fitting than to compare her to a star which sends forth its rays without being changed, even as the Virgin brought forth her Son without loss of bodily integrity. The ray takes nothing from the light of the star, nor does the birth of the Son detract from the integrity of the Virgin. She is, therefore, this radiant Star of Jacob whose rays light up the entire universe." — St. Bernard.

* * *

St. Bernard of Clairvaux (1090-1153). Cistercian Abbot, consumed by sickness and austerity, he died August 20, 1153. He was declared a Saint by Alexander III, Jan. 18, 1174, and proclaimed a Doctor of the Church by Pius VIII in 1830. He is well known among the Doctors of the Church for his profound theological understanding of the function of Mary in Catholic dogma and particularly in the work of the Redemption. He wrote so beautifully and so sweetly about the Blessed Virgin, that he came to be known as *Doctor Mellifluous* and *Mary's singing canary*. To him are attributed two of the best known prayers in the whole Church: the *Memorare* (Remember) and the *Salve Regina* (Hail Holy Queen).

St. Bernard loved Mary tenderly, and his expressions of love towards her are frequently quoted in Marian sermons, as, for example, the following:

O you who flounder amid the vicissitudes of life, as on the waves of a stormy sea, do not divert your eyes from Mary, Star of the sea!

If the winds of temptation blow about you, if your frail bark is hindered by the rocks of tribulations, look to the Star, invoke Mary!

If you are tossed by the waves of pride or ambition, of slander or envy, look at the Star, invoke Mary!

If anger or avarice or sensuality rock the tiny vessel of your heart, look at Mary!

If you are troubled by the enormity of your sins and are on the verge of sliding into the abyss of discouragement, think of Mary!

In dangers, in afflictions, in critical moments, remember Mary, call upon Mary!

Never permit her name to be far from your lips; may the thought of her be always fixed in your heart!

By following her, you can never go astray; by praying to her you will never fall; by thinking of her you will never err; protected by her, you need not fear; guided by her, you will reach salvation.

* * *

"If you do not want a refusal, entrust to Mary's care everything that you want to offer to God." — St. Bernard.

"The sum total of the love of all mothers for their children can never equal the love Mary has for only one soul." — St. Alphonsus Liguori.

* * *

St. Alphonsus Liguori, theologian, founder of the Congregation of the Holy Redeemer, bishop, was born Sept. 27, 1696 and died August 1, 1787. He was declared a Saint by Gregory XVI May 26, 1839 and proclaimed a Doctor of the Church by Pius IX in 1871. Pius XII made him patron of confessors and moralists on April 26, 1950.

St. Alphonsus loved Mary very much; in fact the Virgin Mary appears in all his spiritual works. To her he devoted the most elaborate of his books, *Le Glorie di Maria* (The Glories of Mary), which is one of the great works of Catholic Mariology. This classic book explains, through thousands of sayings, from Saints, ascetic writers and theologians, the popular prayer *Salve Regina* (Hail Holy Queen).

St. Alphonsus firmly established the role of Mary in the history of salvation and solidly based devotion to her on theology. By the grace of the Redeemer, immaculate in her conception, Mary directly cooperated in the redemption of the world effected by Jesus on Calvary: she is the Co-redemptress and consequently the universal, but not exclusive, mediatrix of grace. Through her, one obtains especially the grace of prayer.

St. Alphonsus considered authentic devotion to Mary an assurance and a sign of salvation.

Le Glorie di Maria had an enormous influence on the 19th century and contributed to the great development of Marian devotion at that time and certainly also in the times to come. Allow me now to present to you some quotations from this book:

"It is the will of God that all graces should come to us by the hands of Mary. Now, this is indeed a most consoling truth for souls tenderly devoted to our most Blessed Lady, and for poor sinners who wish to repent . . . . It was on Mount Calvary that Mary began, in an especial manner, to be the Mother of the whole Church . . . . The Blessed Virgin is so great and sublime, that the more she is praised the more there remains to praise . . . . Let us, therefore, always with our hearts and tongues honor this Divine Mother, in order that we may be conducted by her into the kingdom of the blessed."

* * *

"No true devotee of Mary will be damned, because she is the terrible conqueror of the devil." — St. Alphonsus Liguori.

11: May   MONTFORT'S "TRUE DEVOTION TO MARY"

"We ought to perform all our actions through Mary, with Mary, in Mary in order to perform them better through Jesus, with Jesus, in Jesus." — St. Louis de Montfort.

* * *

St. Louis Marie De Montfort (1673-1716), is the founder of the Missionaries of the Company of Mary (Montfort Fathers) and the Daughters of Wisdom. He spent most of his life preaching and writing. A great lover of Mary, he wrote a treatise on Mary, which was discovered and printed in 1842, under the title *The True Devotion to the Blessed Virgin Mary.* In this book, the author gives us a full explanation of the great secret of achieving union with Christ and a tender devotion to Mary. He explains that the foundation for devotion to her is her role in the economy of salvation as mother and queen; that total consecration accompanies the formal and active recognition of the role that Mary plays in human lives, a recognition that entails the renewal of baptismal promises. Montfort advocates the surrender to Christ through Mary of the value of all good actions, past, present, and future, so that they may be used in any way God wishes. Pope Pius XII declared Louis Marie De Montfort a Saint July 20, 1947, and declared his doctrine "burning, solid and correct."

Let me quote for our own spiritual edification a few sayings on Mary of this great Marian writer:

"God gathered together all the waters of earth and called them seas. He gathered together all the graces of Heaven and called them Mary.

"When will it happen that souls will inhale Mary as bodies the air? At that time she will accomplish marvelous works in them.

"No one can acquire an intimate union with Jesus and a perfect fidelity to the Holy Spirit without being greatly united to Mary.

"Mary is the echo of God. If we say 'Mary,' she will answer 'God.' For this reason, union with her is always followed by union with God.

"A lover of Mary must be pious. Mary lived in continual prayer; her devotee must pray and pray continually.

"Mary is so powerful against the devil that he fears a single breath of hers more than all the prayers of the Saints."

* * *

"The Holy Spirit, upon entering a soul and finding there Mary, His beloved Spouse, communicates His life to that soul and fills it with gifts." — St. Louis M. De Montfort.

19

12: May   POPE PAUL VI, A GREAT MARIOLOGIST

"Devotion to the Blessed Virgin Mary is an indication of the Church's genuine piety. This devotion fits into the only worship that is rightly called 'Christian' because it takes its origin and effectiveness from Christ, finds its complete expression in Christ, and leads through Christ in the Spirit to the Father." — Paul VI in *Marialis Cultus.*

* * *

Pope Paul VI (1963-1978) is recognized as the greatest Mariologist in modern times. On February 2, 1974 the whole Catholic world received one of the greatest papal Documents on Mary, entitled *Marialis Cultus.* The theme of this Apostolic Exhortation is "For the right ordering and development of Devotion to the Blessed Virgin Mary." We like to reproduce in this page a few quotations from this very important and fundamental Document. May these few thoughts, and eventually the reading of the Exhortation in its entirety, help us to clarify our way of praying and honoring our Blessed Mother, strengthening and increasing our love toward Her.

"The Blessed Virgin's role as Mother leads the People of God to turn with filial confidence to her who is ever ready to listen with a mother's affection and efficacious assistance. Thus the People of God have learned to call on her as the Consoler of the afflicted, the Health of the sick, and the Refuge of sinners, that they may find comfort in tribulation, relief in sickness and liberating strength in guilt . . .

"The Blessed Virgin's exemplary holiness encourages the faithful to 'raise their eyes to Mary who shines forth before the whole community of the elect as a model of the virtues.' It is a question of solid, evangelical virtues: faith and the docile acceptance of the Word of God; generous obedience; genuine humility; solicitous charity; profound wisdom; worship of God . . . ; her fortitude in exile and in suffering; her poverty reflecting dignity and trust in God . . . ; her virginal purity; her strong and chaste married love. These virtues of the Mother of God will also adorn her children who steadfastly study her example in order to reflect it in their own lives."

* * *

"Devotion to the Mother of the Lord becomes for the faithful an opportunity for growing in divine grace . . . For it is impossible to honor her who is 'full of grace' without thereby honoring in oneself the state of grace, which is friendship with God, communion with Him and the indwelling of the Holy Spirit . . . Mary shows forth the victory of hope over anguish, of fellowship over solitude, of peace over anxiety, of joy and beauty over boredom and disgust, of eternal vision over earthly ones, of life over death." — Paul VI in *Marialis Cultus.*

20

13: May QUEEN OF APOSTLES AND OF ALL APOSTOLATES

"What is the devotion that should be spread throughout the world? Give the most beautiful titles to Mary . . . But the title that will explain all the others, the dignity that serves all her privileges, the office for which she was clothed in the highest virtues is that of being an Apostle . . . All of the most beautiful titles given to Mary are fine. But the one that completes them and explains her most of all is the title of 'Queen of Apostles.'" — Rev. James Alberione.

* * *

Pope Paul VI called the Rev. James Alberione, SSP (1884-1971), "One of the marvels of this century"; and I will not hesitate to call him "The St. Paul of the twentieth century." He is the founder of the Pious Society of St. Paul (1914), of four Congregations of Nuns and of four Secular (Aggregated) Institutes, which constitute the "Pauline Family." No other founder in the whole Catholic Church was so prolific as Father Alberione. Aim of these foundations is the spreading of the Word of God through the modern media of social communication. The Cause of Beatification of this great Servant of God was officially introduced June 19, 1982. In his extensive writings and preachings, Fr. Alberione emphasized, and practiced himself, two very important Devotions: to Jesus the Divine Master, Way, Truth and Life, and to Mary Queen of the Apostles.

Quotations from the writings of Fr. Alberione on the Queen of Apostles:

"The earliest devotion to Mary was practiced by Jesus: He called her mother, obeyed her and loved her. The second devotion to Mary, and the oldest in the Church, was that practiced by the Apostles. The title 'Queen of the Apostles' is the first of all the titles after that of the Divine Maternity . . . . Everything that was given to Mary was to make her an apostle. Her very maternity involved the giving of Jesus; it was her apostolate: give Jesus to the world . . .

"Why did the Lord make Mary so great? Why did He make her the Mother of God and of the Church? Perhaps because the Queen of Apostles is the true Apostle. So the same dignity of Mother of God is related to the Apostles' office: to give Jesus to the world."

* * *

"The first great gift received by the Church was the descent of the Holy Spirit. Mary obtained this in the Cenacle. And as she drew down this first grace of the Holy Spirit among the Apostles, so she acquired almost by right the effusion of the Holy Spirit among souls. Mary is therefore the Sanctifier of our souls." — Rev. James J. Alberione.

14: May   A WHITE CLOUD SEEN FROM MT. CARMEL

"All the prophets desired Mary; let us, too, desire her and pray to her." — Rev. James Alberione.

* * *

Although there are many forms of devotion to Our Blessed Lady, we have to recognize the fact that the oldest is that of Our Lady of Mt. Carmel.

It is believed that the Blessed Virgin was honored many centuries before her birth, and was symbolized in a little shining white cloud (seen by the prophet Elijah) that expanded rapidly over all the blue sky and brought a most needed rain over the land scourged by three years of persistent drought.

The Breviary, in fact, following the lead of ancient tradition, states that on Pentecost Sunday, devoted followers of the prophets Elijah and Elisha, who had been prepared for the coming of the Messiah through the words of the Baptist, immediately embraced the faith of the Gospel, and began to venerate the Blessed Virgin with such affection that, before anyone else, they erected a little Chapel to the purest of Virgins on that very same spot of Mt. Carmel where Elijah had seen the rising little cloud, in the form of a foot. Most probably these followers of Elijah had the opportunity to see and converse with the Blessed Virgin. People started calling them the "Hermits of St. Mary," and, coming together several times a day, they honored the Blessed Virgin with pious practices.

The Carmelite Order continued the tradition of these hermits. In 1245, St. Simon Stock, a Superior General of this Order, in a vision, received from Our Blessed Mother a brown *scapular* with these words: "Wear it, and by means of this scapular I establish an eternal pact of alliance and peace between myself and men, and, provided they are faithful to me, I promise them certain deliverance from dangers, protection in this life and immortal glory in the next."

After the Blessed Virgin appeared again to Pope John XXII, with the promise of shortening the time of suffering in Purgatory for her devotees, this devotion increased tremendously. People of every age, sex, and condition, Popes, cardinals, kings and princes had themselves invested with the holy scapular.

Wearing the scapular (or a medal) after being duly invested, leading a good Christian life, praying every day to Mary will obtain for us the promises of Our Lady of Mt. Carmel.

* * *

"Final perseverance is the crown of all graces; it is the grace of graces. Let us constantly ask it of Mary, honored under the title of Our Lady of Mt. Carmel." — Rev. John Ferraro.

22

15: May   GUADALUPE, THE LADY OF THE AMERICAS

"Mary's Shrines are cities of refuge where we find escape from temptations, and from the punishments we deserve for our sins." — St. John Damascene.

* * *

Our Lady of Guadalupe is the heavenly Patroness of all the Americas. The important thing to remember about this authentic apparition is that Mary is our Mother, that she has a concern and compassion for us, and that she is a person of her word. She did not tell people to do anything, but to come to her, so that she could shower her favors and the blessings of Our Lord upon them.

At daybreak on December 9, 1531, a recently converted Indian peasant named Juan Diego was on the way to Tlatelolco to assist at Mass. When he reached the foot of Mount Tepeyac he heard sublime, joyous melodies that seemed to come from Heaven. In amazement he lifted his glance to the hill from which the celestial music seemed to be coming, and he beheld a pure white cloud over which there rose a glorious rainbow. While the good Juan Diego ecstatically watched the spectacle, he heard a voice call him by name. It urged him to hasten on.

As he hurriedly left the mount in obedience to the command, he saw a woman of divine beauty standing in the midst of the light. Her countenance was as resplendent as the sun, and rays of dazzling light departed from her robe.

"Juanito, dear Juan Dieguito, my son, whom I love tenderly, where are you going?"

He said: "Beloved Lady, I am going to Tlatelolco to assist at Mass which is being celebrated in Mary's honor."

The Lady said: "I praise your devotion, littlest of my sons, and your humility of heart pleases me. I want you to know for certain that I am the perfect and perpetual Virgin Mary, Mother of the true God . . . I wish and intensely desire that in this place a church be erected. Here I will demonstrate, I will exhibit, I will give all my love, my compassion, my help and my protection to the people. I am your merciful Mother. The "little Mother" (Mamacita), of all of you who live united in this land, and of ALL MANKIND, of all those who love me, of those who seek me, of those who have confidence in Me. Here I will hear their weeping, their sorrow, and will remedy and alleviate all their sufferings."

After the miracle of the image of Mary which appeared on Juan Diego's rough cloak, the Bishop finally decided to build the Church that Mary wanted, which became a center of devotion for millions of people.

* * *

"Mary, Mother of God and my tender Mother, pray to Jesus for me."
— St. Philip Neri.

23

16: May   THE BEAUTIFUL LADY OF MASSABIELLE

"A lover of Mary must be pure: 'The immaculate One does not bestow her favors on impure and sensual souls.' " — Rev. J. Ferraro.

* * *

Bernadette Soubirous, a 14 year old humble peasant girl was the recipient of the unique, great privilege of seeing, talking and being the confidant of the most beautiful Lady that appeared to her eighteen times starting February 11, 1858 at the Grotto of Massabielle in Lourdes.

Bernadette herself, in a letter, tells us what happened at the Grotto: "I had gone down one day with two other girls to the bank of the river Gave when suddenly I heard a kind of rustling sound. I turned my head toward the field by the side of the river but the trees seemed quite still and the noise was evidently not from them. Then I looked up and caught sight of the cave where I saw a lady wearing a lovely white dress with a bright belt. On top of each of her feet was a pale yellow rose, the same color as her rosary beads.

"At this I rubbed my eyes, thinking I was seeing things, and I put my hands into the fold of my dress where my rosary was. I wanted to make the sign of the cross but for the life of me I couldn't manage it and my hand just fell down. Then the lady made the sign of the cross herself and at the second attempt I managed to do the same, though my hands were trembling. Then I began to say the rosary while the lady let her beads slip through her fingers, without moving her lips. When I stopped saying the Hail Mary, she immediately vanished . . . I came back next Sunday, feeling myself drawn to the place . . .

"The third time I went the lady spoke to me and asked me to come every day for fifteen days. I said I would and then she said that she wanted me to tell the priests to build a chapel there. She also told me to drink from the stream . . .

"I went back each day for fifteen days and each time, except one Monday and one Friday, the lady appeared and told me . . . to see that the priests build a chapel there. I must also pray for the conversion of sinners . . . Finally, with outstretched arms and eyes looking up to heaven, she told me she was the Immaculate Conception."

Bernadette died a nun in 1879 at the age of 35 after suffering unbearable pains. Mary had told her that she would not make her happy in this world, but in the next. Bernadette died smiling at Mary, who appeared to her for the last time. Pope Pius XI declared her a Saint in 1933. Her body, intact and incorrupt, is buried in the Basilica of Lourdes.

* * *

"Whoever dies in Mary's embrace will awake in the embrace of the Lord." — G. Roschini.

17: May FATIMA, THE DEVOTION OF THE 20th CENTURY

"O my Jesus, forgive us our sins, save us from the fire of hell, lead all souls to heaven, especially those in great need." — Mary to the children of Fatima.

* * *

I am deeply convinced that the full understanding of the Message of Fatima, and putting into action what Mary requested, plus a true and sincere practice of the devotions suggested by Our Lady could heal the evils of the present time, save many souls from eternal damnation and preserve the world from destruction.

Mary appeared in our twentieth century to save the century. The Devotion to Our Lady of Fatima should, therefore, be the devotion of this century.

When did Our Lady appear? From May to October 1917, on the 13th day of each month (except for August when the phenomenon of the sun occurred on the 19th).

Where did Our Lady appear? At the Cova de Ira, in the village of Fatima, Portugal.

The Lady: Our Lady of the Rosary.

The children: Lucy dos Santos (born in 1907 and still living). She has devoted her whole life to prayer and penance, living in the contemplative Carmel community at Coimbra. Popes Paul VI and John Paul II invited her to come to Fatima as a pilgrim and talk to them. — Francesco Marto (1908-1919), died as a young person. He was Eucharistic-centered and spent many hours in prayer before Jesus in the Blessed Sacrament, continually saying the Rosary over and over again because the Blessed Mother had said to him that he must pray many Rosaries before he could go to heaven. — Jacinta, sister of Francesco (1910-1920), died also at a young age, but she was filled with the wisdom of the Spirit and was holy beyond many who lived a long life.

The Message: it is directed to the whole world. Mary is asking us to do something, chiefly: conversion to a better life and repentance for our sins and sins of the world, recitation of the Rosary daily, the fostering of a spirit of sacrifice in accepting sufferings, the love of the Most Holy Eucharist, the consecration of each person and the world (especially of Russia) to Her Immaculate Heart.

The Secret: not officially revealed by the Popes, but, it seems, that it involves destructive wars and great sufferings for the Church and Pope.

* * *

"What a joy it would be to the world and to individual souls if we would ever seek to know Mary better, to love her more ardently, and to give ourselves totally to her so that she may bring us ever closer to her Divine Son." — Cardinal John J. Carberry.

18: May   MARY'S IMMACULATE HEART WILL THRIUMP

*"We believe that all humanity must flee to this port of salvation —
the Immaculate Heart of Mary . . . Men must take refuge in this for-
tress, must trust in this sweet Heart which, in order to save us, asks only
prayer and penance, asks only cooperation."* — Pope Pius XII, 1954.

* * *

The Heart of Mary is the masterpiece of creation, the masterpiece
of the Redemption, the masterpiece of sanctification; it is the Heart that,
in a certain manner, borders upon the confines of divinity. St. John Chrysostom says that "Mary's Heart is the abyss of mysteries." St. Peter Damian
calls it "the sacred treasure of divinity's fullness." St. Epiphanius calls it
"the treasury of the Church." St. Bernardine of Siena describes it as
"the furnace of divine love."

A great battle is on today in the Church. On one side Satan with
a great number of emissaries, all enemies of the Church; on the other
side Mary of the Immaculate Heart and us, the People of God.

The aims of this war: the devil wants the destruction of the Church
and of its members; Mary wants a general return to God through the
practice of a more Christian life, based on love, and the conversion of
Russia.

The victory is undoubtedly ours, through the consecration to the Immaculate Heart of Mary. Are we ready to enlist in the army of Mary and
fight unto victory?

It is evident that we are at the point in the history of the Church
where Mary is to crush the head of Satan. This will be brought about
through the reign of her Immaculate Heart. When people recognize that
peace, hope, and love will come through her, then we will see these things
happen.

The devil is trying everything to destroy anything that is good
through immorality, destruction of families, pornography, dishonesty,
crimes, dissension in parishes and religious communities. He is even instiga-
ting false apparitions to draw the people's attention away from the true apparitions of the Blessed Virgin.

We must do our best to counteract the devil's actions. If we have
devotion to our Mother Mary she will bring about the interest of God
in the lives of all. The consecration of each one of us to Her and our
prayers will give her the power of the Holy Spirit to pierce the darkness that
envelopes the world and give us a tremendous victory over the devil.

* * *

*"Your Heart, O Mary, is of spotless purity . . . the fount of all
benefits and blessings."* — St. John Damascene.

"O Mary, you are the staircase by which God descended to us and by which we must ascend again to Him." — St. Bonaventure

* * *

After God, the Blessed Virgin Mary means everything to me.

God offers me salvation, and if I try during my life to know Him better, serve Him faithfully, and love Him with all my heart, He promises me an eternal reward.

Mary, if I love her, try to imitate her virtues, and pray to her here on earth, will help me to obtain the sanctification and salvation of my soul, will lead me to God, and open for me the gates of Heaven.

Mary, because of her merits and holy life, is for me an *inspiration*. She can help me to do something worthwhile in my life, and to make a somebody of myself at the service of God.

In the midwestern frontiers of America, a dying mother once counseled her little son: "The confusions of life and the noises of the world with their deafening and persistent voice will attempt to destroy all memory of me and these words of your mother. But I will come so close to you and whisper the name of God and remind you of His infinite love so forcibly and sincerely that you will not easily forget it or have it silenced in your soul. Abe, be a somebody; make something of yourself!" Thus spoke the mother of Abraham Lincoln, the man who, although thinking himself a failure, accomplished so much, and became the sixteenth President of the United States.

Mary means to me a *Mediatrix of graces, a Protection.* St. Bernard said that we have need of a Mediator, with the Mediator Himself, and that is Mary, who is the most capable of filling that charitable office. She accepts our recourse to her; she embellishes our works, adorning them with her own merits and virtues, and she presents them to God for the eternal reward.

As Mary protected Jesus, as she protected the Church from its beginning, continues to protect her now, and will continue to protect her till the end of time, she protects me from the snares of the devil and the enemies of my soul, from the destructive force of bad habits and evil inclinations and from every kind of sin. She guides me, with her example, in the acquisition of Christian virtues. She protects me from physical dangers and inspires me how to serve and please God. Yes, Mary means all this to me and much more!

* * *

"Be for us, O Mary, the bright moon in the night of exile, the luminous dawn in the morning of eternity, splendid sun on the day of the Beatific Vision!" — Abbot Cellense.

27

20: May "...I NEED A MOTHER SO MUCH! "

" 'BLESED ARE YOU, O MARY!' . . . This greeting unites millions of hearts . . . Mary is not only the solicitous Mother of men, of peoples, of emigrants; she is also the model of the faith and of the virtues which we must imitate during our earthly pilgrimage . . ." — Pope John Paul II at the Shrine of Our Lady of Guadalupe, Mexico.

* * *

Our mothers brought us into this world . . . Our Blessed Mother Mary, if we love her, will lead us to God and bring us into a world of eternal happiness, Heaven.

A young boy lost his mother and was so disoriented and unhappy that he started looking everywhere for another mother, saying with big tears in his eyes: "I need a mother so much!"

A good neighbor, seeing the poor orphan so unhappy, tried to comfort him the best way possible by telling him: "I know where you would find a beautiful Lady, who will be very happy to have you as her son, and love you very much. Go to the church, she is there waiting for you."

In his great desire of finding a mother, the innocent young orphan believed the good neighbor, and with a smile on his face and a great hope in his heart, ran to the church. He looked everywhere: in the pews, in every corner, at every altar, but no lady . . . A parish priest saw him and asked him gently: "Son, what are you looking for?" The boy timidly answered: "Somebody told me that I would find a nice lady here in the church, who will accept to be my mother. I am an orphan, and I need a mother so much!"

"Come with me, son, and I will introduce you to the most beautiful mother in the world; she will accept you as a son, comfort you, take care of you and love you."

The good priest took the hand of the boy and led him in front of a beautiful statue of Our Lady, and said: "Son, there is your Mother! Love her, and she will love you even more than your mother."

The boy wiped his tears, and, for the first time in many months, smiled at Mary, and Mary smiled back at him.

"Mother" is the most beautiful, the most meaningful, the most sacred name in the world. We all need two mothers: our natural mother and a Spiritual Mother, Mary. All humanity, all of us, "poor children of Eve . . . living in this valley of tears," at all ages need a maternal heart, because we all feel the imperious need of emptying into it, with unlimited trust, all our anxieties, all our hopes.

* * *

"I love Mary, I cannot live without her: she is my real mother; the other mother is only my nurse!" — St. Joseph da Copertino.

21: May   JUDAS' MISTAKE AND SATAN'S COMPLAINT

"However great a man's sins may be, if he shall return to me, I am ready instantly to receive him. Nor do I regard the number or the enormity of his sins, but the will with which he comes to me; for I do not disdain to anoint and heal his wounds, because I am called, and truly am, the mother of sinners." — Our Lady to St. Bridget.

* * *

Judas Iscariot, the betrayer of Our Lord, made two mistakes: in desperation, he forgot that Jesus would have forgiven him if he repented; secondly, it did not come to his mind that Mary, the Mother of Jesus, could have helped him.

The devil complained many times to God that His Mother was stealing so many sinners from him, and that he himself did not have a chance to have recourse to the refuge of sinners.

At the Lenten rendition of the Passion Play, a little seven-year-old girl was seated next to her mother in the middle of a packed hall, completely absorbed by the drama.

The play reached its tensest and most tragic part when the actor who took the role of Judas, going into utter despair after becoming aware of his crime, shrieked at the top of his voice in the most doleful and distressing strain: "To whom can I go? I have betrayed my God! To whom can I go?"

The little girl felt sorry for the wretched man in his terrible plight, and eager to help him out of it, she said to her mother in a childish voice that was audible in the hushed attitude of the audience throughout the entire hall: "Mama, why doesn't he go to Mary?"

The child's simple solution was correct. Had Judas, in his remorse, but gone to Mary and asked her to intercede for him with her Son, instead of becoming a desperate suicide, he could have become a great saint.

Even Satan is jealous of us because we have such a merciful and powerful Mother. It is said that one day the devil said to the saintly Curè ōf Ars (who so greatly loved the Blessed Virgin and made her well known and loved by others), "Ah! If only I had had a Mother like yours, such a merciful refuge of sinners! . . ."

Mary is truly the Mother and the Refuge of sinners! She takes a great pleasure when two brothers, two of Her sons, Jesus and the sinner reconcile. Do you think that you are a great sinner? Listen to what the saintly Blosius said: "There is no sinner so spoiled and so sunken in vice that Mary would detest him and deny him aid."

* * *

"Mary, the Mother of Mercy, has such a desire to save sinners, that she looks for them in order to help them." — St. Alphonsus.

22: May   MARY, MOTHER AND REFUGE OF SINNERS

"Just as the devil always goes in search for someone to devour, so Mary is always looking for someone she can help in any way" — Pope St. Leo the Great.

* * *

Unfortunately, and because of our weak and corrupted nature, we are all sinners. But, fortunately, most of us do not love sin, do not want to continue living in sin, do not intend to offend God deliberately. And so we pray God, continuously, to deliver us from sin, and ask Our Lady to protect us from sin, and pray for us sinners.

But there are many sinners who do not have the will to stop sinning, who, because of the great number and seriousness of their sins, do not have the strength to get out of their miserable condition, and do not have the courage to take the remedies which will help them, and so they fall into despair. God does not want the death of the sinner, and Mary knows that, and she wants to cooperate with God, in every way possible, in saving sinners. She wants to be called the Merciful Mother and Refuge of all sinners.

Mary gave us Jesus, who was to deliver us from sin and Satan. Mary sees in us souls that have been purchased at the price of the death of her Son. Mary well knows that her Son came into the world only to save us poor sinners, as He himself declared: "I am come to save what was lost; . . . the sick people are those who need the doctor."

"Who," exclaims St. Antoninus, "can ever form an idea of the tender care that this loving mother takes of all of us, offering and dispensing her mercy to every one?" Our good heavenly Mother desires the salvation esepecially of those who have left God, the sinners. "It is evident," says St. Bernard, "that she was solicitous for the whole human race."

Mary even anticipates those who have recourse to her by making them find her before they seek her. "The love that this good Mother bears us is so great," says Richard of St. Lawrence, "that as soon as she perceives our want she comes to our assistance. She comes before she is called."

Concluding: Sinners, have no fear! Go to the Refuge of sinners if your own sinfulness tends to crush you. Go to the Refuge of sinners if you are concerned about erring members of your family, or about dear friends. Pray often and confidently: "Holy Mary, Mother of God, pray for us sinners, now and at the hour of our death."

* * *

"If Mary was made Mother of God on account of sinners, how can I, however great my sins may be, despair of pardon?" — St. Anselm.

23: May MARY COMFORTS US IN ALL OUR AFFLICTIONS

"For all who suffer or work, the Blessed Virgin is a sweet repose, a consolation that relieves the afflicted, a medicine for the sick, a safe harbor for the shipwrecked, and a solicitous assistance for all who invoke her." — St. John Damascene.

* * *

By the disobedience of Adam and Eve, tribulation came into this world. Many sufferings will accompany us "poor children of Eve" while passing through "this valley of tears," till we offer our life, in a spirit of sacrifice, to God, at the time of our death.

Hours of trials, when the heart seems to break to pieces, will appear, sooner or later, in our life. To accept the will of God becomes, most of the time, very hard. Who will help us in these very difficult contingencies? There is a Heart, which was pierced many times like ours, a heart full of love and mercy ready to help. It is the heart of the Sorrowful Mother, the "Comforter of the Afflicted."

Mary is the comforter of all humanity. — She is the great Woman, promised by God, who was to crush the infernal enemy's head; the new Eve, who was to repair the ruin caused by the first Eve and cure poor humanity. Guilty, miserable and suffering, man turned to her from the very beginning, uplifting tear-filled eyes and oppressed heart. Mary rose, as beautiful as the dawn, to help and console afflicted humanity.

Mary is the comforter of the Church. — She conversed with the Apostles and the early faithful; she saw her own Son in them. She prayed for all who suffered; she was the Consolatrix of the Church.

Mary is the comforter of individual faithful. — The history of thousands of Shrines and millions of *ex voto* offerings reveals this to us. How many tears are wiped away, how many spiritual and even temporal wounds are medicated, treated and healed! Innumerable souls have stretched out their beseeching hands to Mary in these Shrines; they have trustingly invoked her in their sorrows, in their dangers, and they have been heard. Many great Saints in their deep anguish, in many interior afflictions, in physical and material needs experienced the help and comfort of Mary!

Mary sees our afflictions; Mary feels them in her most sensitive heart; Mary is an all-powerful intercessor before her adorable Son; Mary wants to console everyone. According to St. Anselm, "She is the solace of the afflicted." There is a remedy for every affliction: Mary; and if we invoke her, she will be present to comfort and help us, always.

* * *

"Mary, Comforter of the Afflicted, pray for us!" — Litanies of B.V.M.

31

24: May   MARY, HELP OF CHRISTIANS, CARES FOR US

"Above all else, in union with the Christian people, we issue an invitation to greater fervor in praying to the Mother of Jesus and Our Mother, Mary, Help of Christians, and Queen of the world." — Pope John XXIII, Sept. 28, 1960.

* * *

As Mary cared for her first-born, Jesus, so she cares for each one of us, as the other children that belong to her too.

As Mary listened to the teachings of Christ, so she cares for the purity of His doctrine against the attacks of the enemies of truth.

As Mary cared for the infant Church, so she cared and defended the Church throughout the centuries, she protects it now and she will continue to protect it until the end of the world.

It is impossible to enumerate all the times Mary has come to the aid of her children. Her graces and favors are without number. The history of the Church gives faithful testimony to Mary's continual protection and assistance against rampant heresies through the centuries. She revived faith, strengthened hope, increased prayer, and raised up learned men to wield the pen in defense of the truth. Naturalism, rationalism, modernism, materialism, and now Communism, seemed about to suffocate every religious sentiment, but through Mary's work all passed and will pass: "You have overcome heresy in the whole world!"

Mary protected nations from destruction and saved their Christian faith. Who saved Europe in 1683 from the Turks? The victory of Lepanto was obtained through the recitation of Mary's Rosary.

Mary is the help of individuals. — She constantly watches over each one of us; she obtains for us graces to avoid falls, to gain strength in tribulations, to overcome the difficulties of life. She aids us in all our necessities.

1) *In temporal needs.* — The Gospel shows Mary's intervention in temporal needs. A splendid example is the event at the marriage feast of Cana. Saints and Founders could tell us of how many times Mary provided the material and financial needs of their congregations.

2) *In spiritual needs.* — Mary is even more solicitous about that which concerns our eternal salvation. She welcomes sinners and obtains for them the grace of conversion, she protects us in temptations, and sustains us in good will. Mary desires our spiritual progress and she is anxious to have us receive a greater share of the fruits of the Redemption. Thus she sustains us in our efforts to attain sanctity; she obtains for us perseverance and she will assist us at the hour of our death.

* * *

"Mary, Help of Christians, pray for us!" — Litanies of B.V.M.

25: May   THE MOST CHARITABLE HEART OF MARY

"Live in Mary's heart, love what she loves, desire what she desires, and you will have peace, joy, and sanctity." — St. John Eudes.

* * *

"Love" is a most used and misused word in the English language. It is right to say that we love God and our souls, that we love people and God's creation, that we love what is holy, good and beautiful. But we should not say that we love animals, that we love money, that we love to eat, drink and make merry . . . We only like all these things. We should never debase the most beautiful word LOVE.

The Blessed Virgin Mary loves and enjoys God; she loves and wants to help us as Children of God; she loves all that is holy, good and beautiful.

Charity is the virtue by which we love God above all things for His own sake, and our neighbor as ourselves for the love of God. It is the most noble and meritorious virtue; it is a gift infused in us by God at Baptism together with faith and hope.

We love both God and our neighbor. These words indicate the object of charity, which is twofold, for it includes God and His infinite perfections, and our neighbor, who is the son of God. "Charity," says St. Augustine, "has two arms: with one it embraces God, with the other, our neighbor."

Mary's charity was the greatest, whether considered with respect to God or to her neighbor. From the first moment of her existence Mary was inflamed with such a deep love of God that it surpassed that of the greatest Saints at the end of their lives. St. Bernardine adds that it even excelled that of all the Angels. St. Anselm states: "Mary's love towards God surpassed the love and sweetness of all other creatures." Mary's love was always constant. Her heart was like the altar upon which a fire burns both night and day. Mary did not love God like other Saints with frequent acts of charity: she loved Him with a sole continual act.

Whoever really loves God cannot help but love his neighbor. Mary loved God more than all the Saints, thus immensely more than all the Saints does she love men, and helps them in every need.

God and Mary will treat us charitably according to the charitableness we have for our neighbor. St. Gregory Nazianzen says that "there is no more effective way for us to obtain Mary's love than by showing charity to our neighbor."

* * *

"Ah! Mary, Queen of love, the most amiable, the most loved and the most loving of all creatures . . . deign to grant me a single drop of your love." — St. Alphonsus of Liguori.

33

26: May   MARY, THE MOST PERFUMED LILY OF PURITY

"With herself Mary was so pure; with God she was most loving; with her neighbor she was most merciful." — St. Gregory.

* * *

We are living, today, in an immoral and depraved world. There is no more love for purity. Everything goes; everything is permissible. Pornographic literature, X-rated films, Radio and Television programs are the daily poisoned food of our minds. It is the sex-revolution time, but to me it is the devil's time. Satan is trying to convince souls that nudity is art and not sin, and that nothing is immoral. Who will save the world from this pernicious evil? Mary, the most pure!

Since the fall of Adam, the senses have been rebellious to reason and, of all virtues, chastity has been the most difficult to practice. St. Augustine rightly says: "Of all the combats in which we are engaged, the most severe are those of chastity; its battles are of daily occurrence, but victory is rare."

Mary, our beloved Mother, is the Virgin of virgins. "With reason," wrote St. Albert the Great, "is Mary called the Virgin of virgins; for she, without the counsel or example of others, was the first who offered her virginity to God."

Mary is a most pure lily, and, as St. Ambrose writes, "she is a heavenly vessel." Mary is purity itself: her heart was so pure and bright that it attracted the gaze of the Lord and made Him decide to choose her as His Mother. St. Ephrem in a discourse on Mary's purity said: "O inviolate, O all pure and chaste Virgin Mary, Mother of God, Queen of the universe, hope of the desperate . . . more sublime than the Angels."

By the word *purity* is meant purity of mind, of heart, of word, of deed; purity of body and soul. This virtue is necessary because impurity is one of the principal causes of damnation. The virtue of purity deserves special praise, for it is a very difficult virtue to practice and is fiercely opposed by the devil and the world. Purity is a rare virtue, it is an heroic virtue. But purity will render us happy; it gives us peace, joy, honor, a good reputation, sanctity, beauty, grace, a long life, and a serene death.

How do we practice purity? Being a delicate virtue, we must have continuous vigilance over the mind, the heart, the eyes, the hearing, and the whole person. We must incessantly pray to Mary and put ourselves under her protective mantle, and pray for God's protection.

* * *

"There are only three ways to conquer impurity: mortification, flight from occasions of sin, love of Mary." — St. Robert Bellarmine.

34

27: May   YOUNG SAINTS WHO GREATLY LOVED MARY

"Mary, I love you, I love you, I love you!" — Last words of St. Bernadette Soubirous.

* * *

We really love Mary if we do something constantly to please her. We are not required to do great things in order to show our devotion to Mary. It is enough to perform little acts of devotion, like saluting an image of Mary, bringing flowers to her altar, naming one of our girls "Mary," wearing Mary's scapular, performing little acts of mortification in her honor; but these little demonstrations of affection must be done CONSTANTLY. For some, more advanced in virtue, it could be the devout recitation of three Hail Marys in the morning and in the evening, asking Mary's protection on the new day, or thanking her for the day just past. For others it could be the daily recitation of the Rosary, or the saying of the Angelus morning, noon and in the evening. For those who wish to advance further in their devotion, it could be the imitation of the virtues of the Blessed Virgin, or of one particular virtue which stands out in her life; or perhaps it could be all of these practices of devotion put together. But what is really important is the constancy which we show in performing these actions pleasing to Mary.

When St. John Berchmans, a young Jesuit Novice, was lying on his deathbed, his superior came to his room, accompanied by all the other Religious living in the house. Kneeling by the side of the dying saint, the superior said to him: "My dear brother, you are at the point of appearing before God; before leaving us, I beg of you to tell us what special devotion we ought to practice in honor of Our Blessed Lady, that we may obtain her protection every day of our life, and in particular at the hour of our death."

The dying saint answered: "Any devotion you choose; but let it be constant!"

St. John Berchmans also declared: "I was not born for present things, but for the future; for these eternal things only, let me live, O Mary, and not for those passing." And "I want to keep my eyes pure so that I can better contemplate the beauty of Mary in heaven."

St. Aloysius Gonzaga made a vow of virginity at the age of nine and kept it throughout his life, because he was so devoted to Mary Most Holy.

St. Therese of Lisieux said: "We do well to speak of Mary's prerogatives, but we must not stop at that. We must make her loved."

* * *

"Mary was born from love, she lived for love, and she died of love . . . She is the Mother of beautiful love." — St. Bernardine of Siena.

28: May   DEVOTION TO THE MOST BLESSED MARY

"Whoever is enamoured of Mary attaches his soul to a steadfast anchor that will draw him to the port of happiness." — St. John Damascene.

* * *

Devotion to Mary is the fragrance of our faith, the heavenly smile to the faithful, the note of joy in our hearts, the dearest throb of our Christian life.

What are the reasons of this Devotion? We love Mary, therefore we are devoted to her. 1) *God has a special love for Mary,* because she is the most beautiful creature, both in the natural and supernatural order. "God loves the Virgin alone more than all the other Saints together," wrote Father Suarez. 2) We are devoted to Mary, because of her *dignity* as the Mother of God, and because of her *sanctity.* 3) We are devoted to Mary because *the Church honored her* through all the centuries; because all the Saints honored and prayed to her. 4) We love Mary because *she loves us* and she showered us with so many graces and benefits, materially and supernaturally speaking. 5) Being devoted to Mary means *being predestined* to heaven. Whoever avoids Mary encounters death; whoever finds Mary finds life.

What are the qualities of true devotion? Our devotion must be: 1) *Interior*: that is, it must begin from our heart and must stem from our esteem for Mary and from our knowledge of her greatness. 2) *Tender*: that is, it must be full of confidence. The soul must have recourse to Mary as to a good and true mother in all its needs with great simplicity, trust and tenderness — in doubts, to be enlightened; in temptations, to be sustained; in weakness, to be strengthened; in falls, to be uplifted; in discouragement, to be encouraged; in scruples, to be freed from them; in crosses and adversities, to be consoled. *Holy*: that is, it must lead the soul to avoid sin and imitate Mary's virtues, especially her profound humility, obedience, faith, constant prayer, purity, ardent charity, heroic patience and angelic sweetness. *Constant*: that is, it must strengthen the soul in virtue and render it courageous in opposing the maxims of the world, the desires of the flesh, and the temptations of the devil; it must be continuous and not just a passing sentiment of the heart. *Unselfish*: that is, it must lead the soul to seek God alone rather than self.

* * *

"A true devotee of Mary does not serve this august Queen because of self-interest but simply because Mary deserves to be served. He does not love her because he hopes to receive favors but because she is amiable. Thus a devotee loves and serves Mary faithfully in aridity as well as in times of sweetness and sensible consolations. "— Rev. James Alberione

29: May   PRACTICES OF DEVOTION THAT PLEASE MARY

*"Heaven rejoices, hell trembles, Satan flees every time I say only:
'Hail Mary!' " —* St. Bernard.

* * *

We honor Mary, and we show our love for Her, not so much by multiplying our pious practices, but rather by doing them well, and persevering in them. Only one practice, even a small one, will suffice, as long as it is constant and united to good works.

Some of the practices honoring God's Mother are:

1) *Recitation of the Rosary.* — This practice was persistently recommended by Our Blessed Virgin herself during her apparitions at Lourdes and at Fatima as a means of repentance and reparation for sins, to obtain the conversion and the salvation of souls, and to receive favors from heaven. This devotion is easy, efficacious, and adapted to all times, places and persons. There is a teaching to extract, a virtue to practice, and a grace to ask in each mystery. Meditation on the mysteries is the most important part of the Rosary.

2) *The Three Hail Marys.* — Recited every day, morning and night. It is a very simple, easy and fruitful practice, which we warmly recommend to every one. St. Matilda, St. Anthony of Padua, St. Leonard of Port Maurice, and St. Alphonsus de Liguori used to recite the three Hail Marys in order to thank the Most Holy Trinity for the privileges granted to the Virgin and to obtain the grace of avoiding sin. Many times, Mary has shown that she was pleased with this little practice by granting singular graces to her devotees.

3) *The Five First Saturdays.* — On December 10th, 1925, at Tuy (Spain), Our Lady appeared to Sister Lucia and said: "Look, my daughter, at my Heart, surrounded with thorns with which ungrateful men pierce me at every moment by their blasphemies and ingratitude. You at least try to console me and say that I promise to help at the hour of death, with the graces necessary for salvation, all those who, on the first Saturday of five consecutive months, shall: a) Confess, receive Holy Communion; b) Recite five decades of the Rosary; c) And keep me company for fifteen minutes while meditating on the fifteen mysteries of the Rosary; d) With the intention of making reparation to my Heart.

4) *Novenas* in honor of Our Lady, prayed to under different titles.

5) *Wearing of Scapulars* (or Medals) to obtain protection from danger, or special spiritual benefits promised by Our Lady.

6) *Recitation of the "Angelus,"* morning, noon, night.

7) *Imitating* Mary's virtues and *promoting* Mary's devotion.

* * *

"Pray the Rosary every day, in order to obtain peace for the world."
— Mary to the children of Fatima.

"The Hail Mary is the hammer which crushes the devil and is the joy of the angels, the melody of the predestined, the canticle of the New Testament." — St. Louis de Montfort.

* * *

After the *Our Father,* the most known and recited prayers in the Church are the ones dedicated to Mary. They are:

HAIL MARY. — This is the most beautiful of all the prayers directed to the Mother of God. It is divided into two parts; the first part can be called *praise* and is composed of the words of the Archangel Gabriel when announcing the mystery of the Incarnation, and Elizabeth's words during Mary's visit. The second part contains a *petition,* and is composed of words of the Church.

Thomas a Kempis wrote: "This is a prayer of few words, but one filled with great mysteries; it is brief to say, but far reaching in power. It is more precious than gold and sweeter than honey: worthy of being incessantly murmured in one's heart and frequently repeated with one's lips." Happy are those actions which are enclosed between two Hail Marys; happy also are those days that begin and end with the Ave; in every temptation, in every danger, in every need always say Hail Mary.

HAIL HOLY QUEEN. — This marvelous prayer is attributed to St. Bernard. The thought which pervades the entire Hail Holy Queen is that Mary was made Queen so that she might place all her power at our service. A single loving glance of hers is enough to give us relief from our ills, or help us overcome all temptations, and to lead us to the vision of Jesus. "Mary," says St. Alphonsus, "is all eyes to discover our infirmities and help us." And St. Bernard: "You are the Queen of Mercy, and I am the most miserable sinner of all. Thus, if I am the most wretched of your subjects, you must take more care of me than of all the others."

MEMORARE. — A well known, brief and very sweet prayer; a prayer full of hope in the powerful intercession of Mary. Attributed to St. Bernard or to Claude Bernard, the "poor priest" from Paris, who popularized it.

THE MAGNIFICAT. — It is Mary's song of thanksgiving and praise for the mighty act that God had wrought in her and for the salvation that he has given to Israel. Widely used in the Liturgy.

Other well known prayers in honor of Mary are *THE ANGELUS* and *THE LITANIES OF LORETO.*

* * *

"My soul proclaims the greatness of the Lord . . . because the Almighty has done great things for me." — Luke 1, 49.

31: May   MARY TALKS TO US... WE TALK TO HER

"Let him be silent concerning your mercy, O Virgin most blessed, if there be one who invoked you in his need and who remembers you to have failed him." — St. Bernard.

* * *

My Son Jesus, just before He died, consigned you to me and asked me to be your Mother, to love you and to help you. I accepted the trust willingly and with great love, because, as I loved Jesus, my Son and my God, so I love all of you as my true children.

Good children listen to their mothers; so, if you love me, listen to what I want to say to you:

1) *Love God* above all things, observe His commandments, do not offend Him by sinning. And if you fall into sin because of your own weakness, remember that I can help you.

2) *Love your neighbor* as yourself, because you are all my children, and I embrace all of you, and my only wish is to see you in the embrace of God, saved in heaven.

3) *Remember to pray.* In prayer you get all the strength you need to face the dangers of life, overcome the temptations of the enemy of your souls, the devil; acquire virtues, and perform many good deeds.

4) *Consecrate* yourselves to my Immaculate Heart, and I will always watch over you, comfort you, and help you in all your needs.

At Guadalupe I told Juan Diego: "My son, where are you going? Which way are you taking? Listen, my son, to what I am telling you now: do not be disturbed; do not be dismayed at anything, not even at illness or any other frightening or sad event . . . Am I not with you, I who am your mother? Have I not placed you under my protection? Am I not your security? I — as your mother — always carry you in my heart and in my arms; therefore, do not be afraid of me!"

I say the same things to you till you will be with me, safe in heaven.

Yes, Blessed Mary, my sweet and powerful Mother, I love you; keep your holy hand upon my head; guard my mind, my heart and my senses, that I be not stained with sin. Sanctify my thoughts, desires, words, and actions so that I may please you and your Jesus, my God, and reach heaven with you. I want to do everything through you, in you and with you. Jesus and Mary give me your holy blessing!

* * *

"Lady, full and overflowing with grace, all creation receives new life from your abundance. Virgin, blessed above all creatures, through your blessing all creation is blessed, not only creation from its Creator, but the Creator himself has been blessed by creation!" — St. Anselm of Aosta.

39

OCTOBER

DEDICATED TO MARY, QUEEN OF THE HOLY ROSARY

1: October   OCTOBER DEDICATED TO THE ROSARY

"Several times during the course of Our Pontificate, We have made known Our predilection for devotion to the Holy Rosary and the great trust We placed in it . . . In our Encyclicals, We abundantly emphasized the reasons for Our predilection and Our trust, and the same reasons impelled Us to prescribe, until further notice, the continuation of the pious exercise of the month of October in honor of the glorious Virgin of the Rosary." — Leo XIII, Letter "Piu' volte," October 31, 1886.

* * *

The month of October is dedicated to Mary, the Mother of God, under the title of "Our Lady of the Rosary." It is a month in which we are encouraged to recite this beautiful prayer both publicly and privately.

The Rosary is truly a Gospel prayer. The mysteries of the Rosary express the joy of the entrance of God into time, the redemptive suffering of Christ, and the glory of the Risen Lord. There is also a meditative element in the careful, prayerful recitation of the Rosary: a quiet rhythm, a lingering pace encourages us to dwell on the events of Our Lord's life through the eyes of Our Lady.

Love of the Rosary and the devout recitation of it through the centuries has been considered a source of inspiration, a sign of victories and a pledge of eternal life. One cannot love the rosary without growing in love of God, one cannot be a client of Mary without love of her Son. Pope Pius XI declared: "I would conquer the world if I had an army which recites the Rosary."

With a Rosary in each hand at the Angelus on Sunday, October 29, 1982, Pope John Paul II said: "Today, the last Sunday of October, I wish to draw your attention to the Rosary. In fact, throughout the whole Church, October is the month dedicated to the Rosary.

"The Rosary is my favorite prayer. A marvelous prayer! Marvelous prayer in its simplicity and in its depth. In this prayer we repeat many times the words that the Virgin Mary heard from the Archangel, and from her kinswoman Elizabeth. The whole Church joins in these words. It can be said that the Rosary is, in a certain way, a prayer-commentary on the last chapter of the Constitution 'Lumen Gentium' of Vatican II, a chapter which deals with the wonderful presence of the Mother of God in the mystery of Christ and the Church."

* * *

"If you desire peace in your hearts, your homes and your country, assemble every evening to recite the Rosary." — Pius IX.

2: October   INVITATION TO PRAY THE ROSARY

"The Rosary is the glory of the Church." — Pope Julius II.

* * *

There are many reasons why we should pray the Rosary, and these reasons are based on four convincing and authoritative sources:

1) *Papal Documents.* — In the last 225 years of Catholic Church history, eighty six Papal Documents came out on the Rosary and the Rosary Devotion, and more pronouncements are due to appear. So we can, with almost absolute certainty, state that there is no other subject that received so much coverage by the Popes, than the Rosary. These Papal Documents should be proof enough to convince us of the great importance of the Rosary Devotion.

2) *Vatican Council II.* — In the *Constitution on the Sacred Liturgy* we read: "Popular devotions of the Christian people are to be highly commended, provided they accord with the laws and norms of the Church, above all when they are ordered by the Apostolic See."

In the very important Document *Constitution on the Church,* Chapter VIII is entirely dedicated to the Blessed Virgin Mary, Mother of God in the Mystery of Christ and the Church, and we read: "Mary, exalted above all angels and men . . . is justly honored by a special cult in the Church."

3) *USA Bishops' Pastoral Letters.* — In *Human Life in Our Day,* 1968, the Bishops stated " . . . We give top priority to whatever may produce a sound 'family spirituality': family prayer, above all that which derives its content and spirit from the liturgy and other devotions, particularly the Rosary." In *Woman of Faith,* 1973 we read: "The Dominican Rosary of 15 decades links our Lady to her Son's salvific career . . . The recommended saying of the Rosary does not come merely in 'telling the beads.'. . . Interwoven with the prayer are the 'meditated mysteries.' "

4) *Desire of Our Lady.* — At Lourdes, 1858, Mary invited Bernadette to say the Rosary, and She recited it with her, "Pray the Rosary in reparation for the sins of the world"

At Fatima, 1917, Mary told the three children, repeatedly: "I am the Lady of the Rosary, continue to pray the Rosary every day . . . Pray the Rosary every day, in order to obtain peace in the world, and the end of the war . . . Go to the Cova da Iria on the 13th of every month to continue praying the Rosary every day."

* * *

"The Rosary is my favorite prayer, a marvelous prayer." — Pope John Paul II.

44

THE ROSARY, A COMPENDIUM OF OUR FAITH

"The Rosary offers an easy way to inculcate the chief mysteries of the Christian religion and to impress them upon the mind." — Encyclical of Pope Leo XIII "Magnae Dei Matris," Sept. 7, 1892.

* * *

Through the Rosary, Mary invites us not only to prayer, but also offers us a simple and effective means of meditation which becomes a compendium of the mysteries we are bound to believe, a way strewn with examples that we should imitate, supernatural life guaranteed to us as a pledge of everlasting life.

To what can all our faith be reduced? To the two principal mysteries of the Unity and Trinity of God and of the Incarnation of Jesus. And here you find these two mysteries unfolding themselves in the recitation of the mysteries of the Rosary.

In the *joyful mysteries* we see the work of the Blessed Trinity in preparing the incarnation of the Word: and then we find delight in the serene vision of the birth and infancy of Our Lord Jesus Christ.

In the *sorrowful mysteries* we follow the bloody stages marked by Jesus in fulfilling the work of our redemption.

And in the *glorious mysteries* we see in the light of a most beautiful reality that blessed and happy life that has been guaranteed us through the passion and death of Our Redeemer.

To meditate lovingly upon these mysteries means to live in the pure light of our faith; it means strengthening our heart with those sweet certainties that rest entirely on the words of Christ and on the salvation He brought to us.

The Most Rev. Bishop Fulton J. Sheen made this beautiful declaration: "When we say the Rosary, we are saying to God, the Trinity, to the Incarnate Savior, to the Blessed Mother: 'I love you, I love you, I love you'!"

* * *

"The Rosary is an excellent means of professing our faith . . . it provides the Christian with sustenance with which to nourish and strengthen his faith . . . . May the august mysteries of our faith penetrate souls more deeply by means of the Rosary, with the happy result that 'we may imitate what they contain and obtain what they promise.' " — Pope Leo XIII.

4: October   **TO JESUS THROUGH MARY'S ROSARY**

"Feeling very keenly the needs of the prayers of Christians, we are aware that of all the forms of prayer, that of the Rosary is more than ever necessary, for it not only addresses itself to her through whom it pleased God to send every grace to us, but more than any other prayer it bears the universal stamp of collective and familial prayer." — Letter of Benedict XV to Rev. C. Becchi, O.P., Sept. 18, 1915.

* * *

To go to God through Mary is the safest and surest way. God made it so when He invited men to the ecstasy of that first adoration in the Grotto of Bethlehem, when Mary presented the God-child to all mankind. He emphasized it at Cana, and confirmed it on Calvary.

St. Louis Marie Grignon De Montfort declared that there is only one way to go to Jesus, and that way is to go through Mary, His Mother. And why? The answer is very simple. God, the Almighty Father, did not find a better way to send His Beloved Son into the world than to pass through Mary.

For liturgical Marian feast days, the Church interprets Sirach 24:11-31 as referring to Mary, in what is called the "accommodated sense" (*sensus plenior*) of scripture. We should be able to find some expressions that serve to emphasize the spiritual value of the Rosary as a way to go to Jesus. "I am the mother of fair love, and of fear, and of knowledge, and of holy hope. In me is all grace of the way, and of the truth, in me is all hope of life and of virtue. Come over to me, all you that desire me, and be filled with my fruits. For my spirit is sweeter than honey, and my inheritance above honey and the honeycomb."

If you pay close attention to the text, you find the three characteristics that Christ accommodates to himself when He said: "I am the way, and the truth, and the life. No one comes to the Father but through me. (John 14, 6). But inasmuch as Christ came to us by way of Mary, and wants us to go to Him by way of Mary, the Blessed Virgin also can, with all good reason, say: "In me is all grace of the way and of the truth, in me is all hope of life and of virtue. Come over to me!"

In saying the Rosary we find the surest way to go to Jesus by the safest way, that is, through Mary.

* * *

"This prayer, the Rosary, is perfect because of the praise it offers, because of the lessons it imparts, because of the graces it obtains and because of the triumphs it achieves." — Pope Benedict XV.

5: October   SAINT DOMINIC AND THE ROSARY

"The Rosary provides the Christian with sustenance with which to nourish and strengthen his faith." Encyclical "Fidentem piumque" by Leo XIII, Sept. 20, 1896.

* * *

It was about the year 1208. St. Dominic, the founder of the Order of Preachers (Dominicans), was engaged in a difficult mission: the conversion of the irreligious and stubborn Albigenses heretics of South France. He had worked with them for fourteen years, preaching to them by day and praying for them by night. Results? Not a single convert. He even engaged other famous preachers to work with him. But, notwithstanding their eloquence and zeal, the results were the same.

Disappointed and discouraged, but still hoping, St. Dominic decided to bring his problems to the Blessed Mother of God. One night, while he was kneeling in the chapel of Notre Dame at Prouille, Our Lady appeared to him — or inspired him — to use a different method, a new approach with the heretics. Instead of depending on the force of eloquence and the presentation of difficult subjects, he decided to select and preach on episodes from the life of Christ, as given to us through the Gospels. After the enunciation of the episode and a short explanatory sermon St. Dominic would invite the people to meditate for a short time on the subject, then draw their own conclusions and make practical resolutions. After this, before continuing with the preaching, came the most important part of the service: Praying. Praying with prayers also taken from the Gospel: the Our Father, the Hail Mary, repeated many times, and concluding glorifying the Blessed Trinity with the Glory . . .

The new Devotion proved to be very efficacious. In fact, armed with his new weapon, St. Dominic worked successfully among the Albigenses, bringing many of them back to the faith.

At the same time, we have the very first military victory obtained through the recitation of the Rosary. Simon de Montfort was asked to organize a military crusade against these same heretics, the Albigenses, who had started a tremendous work of destruction in South France. The Christian army, instructed by St. Dominic, recited the Rosary before the crucial battle of Muret (1213). De Montfort won and ascribed his victory, under God, to the prayers of the Rosary, and built at Muret, in token of his gratitude, the first chapel of the Rosary.

* * *

"Say the entire Rosary well every day; in the hour of death you will bless the moment you chose so holy a resolution." — (St. Louis de Montfort).

47

6: October

WHAT IS THE ROSARY?

"We confidently add our voice to the voices of Our Predecessors that the Christian people individually and jointly, will recite the Rosary ever more habitually, firmly convinced that it is the most beautiful flower of human piety and the most fruitful font of heavenly graces. Being (the Rosary) a prayer of supplication and of intercession, it is undeniably perfect: whether by the praises it addresses and the invocations it expresses, the aid it procures and the teaching it contains, or by the graces and the victories it leads up to." — Pope Benedict XV, in a letter to Rev. C. Becchi, O.P., Sept. 18, 1915

* * *

The word "Rosary" derives from the Latin word "rosarium" meaning a garden of roses, and was used as far back as the thirteenth century.

The Rosary, containing one hundred and fifty Hail Marys, is sometimes called the Psalter of Mary, in imitation of the one hundred and fifty Psalms of David contained in the Bible. The Psalter of David is used by the priest in the breviary, whence the Rosary is called the People's Breviary. It is also referred to as the People's Bible, because its fifteen mysteries unfold to the world God's most sublime revelation — the life of His only begotten Son.

Pope John Paul II declared: "Against the background of the words 'Ave Maria' there pass before the eyes of the soul the main episodes in the life of Jesus Christ. They are composed altogether of the joyful, sorrowful and glorious mysteries, and they put us in living communion with Jesus through — we could say — His Mother's heart.

"At the same time our heart can enclose in these decades of the Rosary all the facts that make up the life of the individual, the family, the nation, the Church and mankind. Personal matters and those of one's neighbor, and particularly of those who are closest to us, who are dearest to us. Thus in the simple prayer of the Rosary beats the rhythm of human life."

* * *

"We are well aware of the Rosary's powerful efficacy to obtain the material aid of the Blessed Virgin. Although there is more than one way of praying to obtain this aid, we nevertheless consider the Rosary the most suitable and most fruitful means." — Encyclical "Ingruentium malorum" of Pope Pius XII, Sept. 19, 1951.

7: October FEAST OF THE MOST HOLY ROSARY

"Experience has shown us that to inculcate love of the Mother of God deeply in souls there is nothing more efficacious than the practice of the Rosary." — Pope Leo XIII.

* * *

The purpose of the Feast of the Most Holy Rosary is to thank God that, through the devout recitation of Mary's Rosary, many victories were obtained against the enemy of God and the Church. The Rosary is also an extremely efficacious means of sanctification and a sure spiritual instrument of victory against Satan, the infernal foe of our souls.

When the Christian faith of all Europe was in extreme danger of being destroyed by the powerful Turkish troops, Pope Pius V exhorted all the faithful to say the Rosary, asking Our Blessed Mother for a victory; he himself did likewise. The small Christian navy, under the leadership of Don Juan of Austria, faced the tremendously powerful Turkish navy at Lepanto. It was Sunday, October 7, 1571. Pope Pius, still with the rosary beads in his hands, opened the window of his room, and saw, in a vision, the smart maneuvers of the Christian forces, destroying, one by one, the ships of the Turks. When the darkness arrived, the Turkish sea power was a thing of the past. Pope Pius joyfully exclaimed: "We have won! Mary's Rosary gave us the victory!"

In memory of the event, he decreed that thanks be rendered to the Blessed Virgin every year on October 7. Two years later (1573), Pope Gregory XIII ordered that the event be solemnized on the first Sunday of October, under the title of "Our Lady of Victory."

After another victory of the Christians over the Turks on August 5, 1716, in Hungary, under Emperor Charles VI, and after the liberation of the island of Corcyra (Corfu'), Pope Clement XI (1700-1721), changed the name of the feast from Our Lady of Victory into the "Feast of the Holy Rosary." Pope Leo XIII (the Pope of the Rosary) established for this Feast a proper Office and Mass, and he added to the Litany of the Most Blessed Virgin the invocation: "Queen of the Most Holy Rosary, pray for us!" Finally Pope Paul VI, on March 5, 1971, decreed that this solemnity be celebrated, in perpetuity, every year on October 7 throughout the Universal Church.

All this was done to perpetuate the memory of the Virgin's protection through the Rosary devotion.

* * *

"The Rosary invites our fingers, our lips, and our heart in one vast symphony of prayer, and for that reason is the greatest prayer ever composed by man." — Bishop Fulton J. Sheen.

8: October   PAPAL DOCUMENTS ON THE ROSARY

"We do not hesitate to affirm that we put great confidence in the Holy Rosary for the healing of the evils that afflict our times. Not with force, not with arms, not with human power, but with divine help obtained through the means of this prayer will the Church be able to confront the infernal enemy." — Encyclical "Ingruentium malorum" of Pope Pius XII, Sept. 19, 1951.

* * *

There are eighty six Papal Documents on the Holy Rosary, between Encyclical Letters, Apostolic Letters, Apostolic Constitutions, Apostolic Exhortations, Letters to special people, Motu Proprios, Allocutions and Radio Messages.

All these Documents represent the thoughts, the teaching and interests of the Church through the voice of eleven Supreme Pontiffs, from Clement XIII to John Paul II, regarding the Devotion to the Holy Rosary.

Three major topics are treated in depth in these Documents: 1) The nature and the history of the Rosary; 2) Efficacy of the Rosary in the life of souls, in serious cases of dangers for the Church and the Christian Doctrine, in ending wars, and in the needs of our time; 3) Devotion to the Holy Rosary.

If so many Popes, through so many Documents, are trying to convince us to recite the Rosary, we should admit that there is something really special, something good in this Devotion.

Cardinal Gabriel-Marie Garrone, in the Preface of a book on the Rosary, wrote these beautiful words: "The Rosary belongs to the Church. When we point out the official testimonies of the Supreme Pontiffs, that is to say their appeals — the word encouragement would not convey their forcefulness — when these appeals which are almost disconcerting by reason of their number, seriousness, and continuity; when we reflect on the long experience of people, or on the supernatural efficacy of the Rosary in reviving and stimulating faith and zeal, then we must truly say that the Rosary belongs to the Church.

"If the Church recommends devotion to the Rosary with such insistence, she does so in undeniable obedience to the trustworthy instinct of her maternity, its educative and nutritive value for faith and charity. In all this the Church clearly has the assurance of guiding her children toward the Truth of which she is the guardian. In all this the Church has the assurance of placing in the hands of her children the good tools of their conversion and sanctification."

* * *

"The Rosary is an excellent means of professing our faith." — Pope Leo XIII.

9: October
THE ROSARY AND THE POPES

"In these last weeks both I and the Holy See had numerous proofs of good will from people in the whole world. I wish to translate my gratitude into decades of the Rosary in order to express it in prayer, as well as in the human manner; in this prayer so simple and so rich."
— John Paul II (Oct. 29, 1978).

* * *

Leo XIII, the Pope who wrote more than any other Pope on the Rosary, in his Letter, "Piu' volte" to the Cardinal Vicar of Rome, on October 31, 1886 declared: "We believe that We never have done enough to promote this pious practice among the faithful. We wish to see it ever more widely diffused so that it may become the truly popular devotion in all places at all times . . .

"Since it is clearly evident that this form of prayer is particularly pleasing to the Blessed Virgin, and that it is especially suitable as a means of defense for the Church and all Christians, it is not at all surprising that several others of Our Predecessors have made it their aim to favor and increase its spread by their urgent admonitions. Thus, Urban VI testified that 'every day the Rosary obtained fresh blessings for Christianity.' Sixtus V decreed that this method of prayer 'redounded to the honor of God and the Blessed Virgin, and was well suited to ward off impending dangers,' and Leo X stated that 'It was instituted to oppose pernicious heresiarchs and heresies'; while Julius II called it 'the glory of the Church.' St. Pius V said that 'with the spread of this devotion the meditations of the faithful have become more ardent and their prayers more fervent, and they have quickly become different people; the darkness of heresy has been dissipated, and the light of Catholic faith has broken forth in renewed glory.' Lastly, Gregory XIII in his turn pronounced that 'the Rosary has been instituted by St. Dominic to appease the anger of God and to implore the intercession of the Blessed Virgin Mary.'"

The Rosary, and all that it implies in love of Christ and His Mother, becomes an intimate part of life; it grows on one imperceptibly; it gives peace and light; it fills the empty heart and consoles the aching one; it is indeed a pledge of eternal life.

* * *

"The Rosary is an excellent prayer, but the faithful should feel serenely free in its regard. They should be drawn to its calm recitation by its intrinsic appeal." (Pope Paul VI, Marialis Cultus).

51

10: October   THE ROSARY, A GOSPEL PRAYER

"Upon arriving, the angel Gabriel said to Mary: 'Rejoice, O highly favored daughter! The Lord is with you. Blessed are you among women.'"
— Gospel of St. Luke, I, 28.

* * *

W. J. Harrington, O.P. in presenting his book "The Rosary: A Gospel Prayer" said: "The Rosary is a thoroughly biblical, a Gospel prayer. The reason it is so is by no means only because the Lord's Prayer and the greatest part of the Hail Mary, come straight from the gospels. It is because almost all the 'mysteries' of the Rosary come straight from the gospels. The Joyful Mysteries are taken from the first two chapters of St. Luke; the Sorrowful Mysteries are based on the passion narrative or the four gospels; and the Glorious Mysteries reflect the close of the gospel and its overflow into the new age of the Spirit and the Church.

"When we look at these mysteries in their Gospel setting, we find that they are Christ-centered. It is a striking fact that the Rosary, the Marian prayer *par excellence,* is taken up almost wholly with the Son of Mary. As the prayer is arranged she is, in a sense, a frame to him — she who once enclosed him in her womb. She does figure in the two first Joyful Mysteries, Annunciation and Visitation, while the last two Glorious Mysteries, Assumption and Queenship, are hers. But in between is all his. The emphasis is as it ought to be.

"Because this prayer is biblical it has its priorities right. We find that the child born of Mary is none other than the Lord, the Savior. Born one of us, he is like us in all things: He suffered and died. The great difference is that 'with his stripes we were healed'; his death won salvation for us. His death was his triumph. The Risen Lord, returned to his Father, his task accomplished, has sent forth the life-giving Spirit. There we have the reality and the purpose of the Incarnation: God became man to make us children of God. 'God sent forth his Son, born of woman . . . that we might receive adoption as sons' (Gal. IV, 4f). The time had fully come. The Rosary is the prayer of the fullness of time."

Pope Paul VI, in "Marialis Cultus," February 2, 1974, said: "The Rosary is a Gospel prayer, as pastors and scholars like to define it . . . As a Gospel prayer, centered on the mystery of the redemptive Incarnation, the Rosary is therefore a prayer with a clearly Christological orientation."

* * *

"Elizabeth was filled with the Holy Spirit and cried out in a loud voice: 'Blest are you among women and blest is the fruit of your womb.'"
— Gospel of St. Luke, I, 41-42.

52

THE ROSARY, A FAMILY PRAYER

"We are persuaded that families will receive from the recitation of the Rosary a guarantee of heavenly blessings . . . When parents and children gather together at the end of the day in the recitation of the Rosary, together they meditate on the example of work, obedience and charity which shone in the house of Nazareth; together they learn from the Mother of God to suffer serenely; to accept with dignity and courage the difficulties of life and to acquire the proper attitude toward the daily events of life." — Letter "We have been informed" by Pope John XXIII to Rev. Patrick Peyton, C.S.C., May 1, 1959.

* * *

Each day of the year, but especially during the month of October, every member of the family should get together for the recitation of the Rosary. The best time is early in the evening, preferably immediately after the meal, before scattering for the evening activities or before your favorite television programs start.

The parents or one of the children (alternating every day) should lead the recitation. You can kneel in front of a statue or a picture of Our Blessed Lady, or sit comfortably.

The Rosary could be a means of tying together, spiritually speaking, and keeping together all the members of the family.

The well-known, Irish-born Father Patrick Peyton, C.S.C., founder of the Family Rosary Crusade said: "When Mary is invited into the home and beseeched repeatedly with the words, 'Pray for us now and at the hour of our death,' she will defend its members and protect them against the overwhelming evils of today at the two most important moments in their lives — now and at the hour of death." The same Father Peyton also declared: "The family that prays together, stays together."

A wish and a blessing from Pope John XXIII: "We wish to invite you to live a Marian life . . . May the family Rosary be a balm of peace for your homes . . . May the Rosary be ever in your hands; may the Marian prayer continue to sanctify your family reunion every night, and may it give the spiritual tone to your whole life"

* * *

"Mary taught Bernadette to say the Rosary. She gently led her from one Ave to the next; she joined her in silence up to the Glory Be which she recited with her . . . The Rosary has something unique, sweet, and dear about it for each one of us. Does it not enable us to draw near to Mary, Our Lady, in a wonderful way and, through her, to draw near to Jesus and to His Heart in an atmosphere that is unique for its purity, fervor and power?" — Card. G. M. Garrone.

12: October
THE ROSARY POINTS THE WAY TO PERFECTION

"The Rosary . . . is also a powerful incentive and encouragement to the practice of Christian virtues, and these it develops and cultivates in our souls. Above all, it preserves and nourishes. our Catholic faith." — Letter "Inclitam ac perillustrem" by Pope Pius XI, March 6, 1934.

* * *

What is Christian life? It is the life of man, enlightened by the knowledge of God, based upon the holy fear of God, upheld by the hope of a reward, and completely vivified by the love of God. Our Blessed Mother, through the Rosary, teaches us to travel and to advance along the path of Christian perfection by unfolding before our eyes pictures of joy, of sorrow, and of glory. Without joy there is no living; it is impossible to live without pure and real joy. And it is this reality of inward and pure joy that is pointed out for us by the Blessed Mother in the joyful mysteries. By meditating on these joyful mysteries, we come to a realization that our faith is a source of joy; and we realize moreover that this joy is all of an inward nature, not subject to the encounters and events of the external world, but vital and perennial.

It is true that this joy does not exclude sorrow; on the contrary, it presupposes and demands it as a counter measure against dissipation, and as a loyal ally that will prepare the soul for the reality of the true glory that will never end. But even in the field of sorrow, which is inevitable, inasmuch as we are members of a fallen race and are merely pilgrims here on earth, think of the enlightenment shed on it by the example of the sufferings both of Jesus and Mary! What comfort is in the thought that they have gone before us suffering immeasurably more than we, although perfectly innocent! What an incentive in facing our trials!

In meditating upon Christ sweating blood in the garden; in meditating upon our Savior scourged and crowned with thorns, and in meditating upon Christ carrying the cross to Calvary and being nailed to the cross out of love for me, what a wonderful source we find of love for us, what a truly wonderful source we find of sincere sorrow and pure, unselfish love! But suffering is a means to obtain eternal glory. For if Christ is risen, then it follows that we shall rise again; by ascending into heaven, he went to prepare a place for us. And He gives a guarantee that it will be so, by pouring forth into our hearts the charity of the Holy Spirit and by crowning His and our Mother there in heaven in order to spur us on to work with generosity towards our sanctification.

* * *

"The Rosary . . . is a form of union with God and has a most uplifting effect on the soul." — Pope John XXIII.

54

13: October

THE ROSARY PRESENTS US WITH A HEAVENLY LIFE

"This simple and profound prayer, the Rosary, teaches us to make Christ the principle and end, not only of Marian devotions, but of our entire life." — Paul VI.

* * *

He who knows how to meditate well on the mysteries of the Rosary, discovers there the very life of heaven itself: "He that shall find me, shall find life, and shall have salvation from the Lord." (Prov. 8, 35). The joyful mysteries teach us and give us a life of intimacy with our Lord: a life of union by means of the divine word that sows in us the great truths and chaste counsels, a life of brotherly love in the bonds of the family and of Christian friendship, a life of actual personal union with Christ when He comes and is reborn within us in Holy Communion, a life of finding Him again, when after we have fallen, we cast ourselves at His feet in the Sacrament of forgiveness.

The sorrowful mysteries teach us, and give us a life of union with Christ in suffering. We should never forget that the duty of every true Christian is, as St. Paul declares: "to fill up in his flesh what is lacking of the sufferings of Christ." And on the other hand, we must remember that when a Christian suffers pain or persecution for the love of Jesus Christ, he is intimately united with his Master. Christ Himself, in fact, says to Saul: "Why are you persecuting me?" And St. Perpetua, while suffering, just before her execution, the pains of childbirth, answers the jailer jeering her about the suffering that awaits her in the arena: "Tomorrow, it will be my Lord who will suffer within me."

The glorious mysteries guarantee us a life of union with God in everlasting glory and give us a foretaste of it in the tender joys of the indwelling of God in our souls, in the gentle outpourings of the Holy Spirit, in those intimate inspirations that let us feel his lifegiving breath, in the ineffable reality of the Mystical Body, in the mysterious relations of the communion of Saints, in the tender atmosphere of love that one enjoys when he really lives his devotion to our gentle and sweet Mother Mary.

See to it that your Rosary, said every day and meditated upon with the heart of a true Christian, makes a crown of lilies and roses blossom forth within you, that will give off perfume toward God and spread an odor of edification round about for the brethren.

* * *

"Place your confidence in the Holy Rosary. Use this most powerful form of prayer wtih the utmost possible zeal, and let it become more and more esteemed." — Pius XII.

55

14: October — THE ROSARY, YESTERDAY AND TODAY

"The Rosary is the Creed turned into prayer." — Card. J. H. Newman

* * *

Thousands of articles and research books discuss the origin and form of the Rosary. Many are the opinions expressed on the subject, but the most logical, it seems, is this: Our Lady inspired St. Dominic to introduce in the Church a new devotion, very pleasing to Mary, called "The Rosary" — heavenly perfumed Prayer-Meditation.

The Devotion of the Rosary grew tremendously through the centuries, and it became, excepting the liturgical eucharistic Mass, the most popular, the number one devotion in the Church. Saints, Popes, kings, theologians and scientists, well educated and common people made the Rosary their favorite devotion.

What happened to the Rosary Devotion in the third quarter of our Century? An unexplainable and tragic decline in its practice, due, maybe, to a new Christian mentality regarding the form of praying today. Some people see in the Rosary only a mechanical and repetitive prayer.

But, let us remember, the Church never changed its mind concerning this wonderful Devotion. Card. G. M. Garrone declared: "The Rosary belongs to the Church because of so many official testimonies of a great number of Supreme Pontiffs of the past and of the modern times."

Thank God that things are changing; there is a sincere and concrete sense of revival on the part of the faithful toward the Rosary Devotion. This revival is strongly supported by the last Popes, through their continuous public Exhortations and Encyclical Letters.

* * *

"We wish, venerable Brothers, to dwell for a moment on the renewal of the practice which has been called 'the compendium of the entire Gospel,' the Rosary. To this Our predecessors have devoted close attention and care . . . We, too, from the first general audience of Our Pontificate on July 13, 1963, have shown our great esteem for the pious practice of the Rosary. Since that time we have underlined its value on many different occasions, some ordinary, some grave. Thus, at a moment of anguish and uncertainty, We published the Letter 'Christi Matri' (Sept. 15, 1966), in order to obtain prayers to Our Lady of the Rosary and to implore from God the supreme benefit of peace. We renewed this appeal in Our Apostolic Exhortation 'Recurrens mensis Octobris' (Oct. 7, 1969), in which We also commemorated the fourth centenary of the Apostolic Letter 'Consueverunt Romani Pontifices' of our predecessor Saint Pius V, who in that document explained and, in a certain sense, established the traditional form of the Rosary." — Paul VI, "Marialis Cultus," Feb. 2, 1974.

15: October   WHEN, WHERE, HOW TO SAY THE ROSARY

"Let the Rosary — this simple beautiful method of prayer enriched with many indulgences — be habitually recited by all and in every home. These are my last words to you, the memorial I leave behind me." — Pius IX.

* * *

The Rosary could be said any time during the day or at night; alone or with another person; as a communal prayer in a group or as a devotional prayer in church.

The Rosary could be recited anywhere: kneeling, standing up or sitting down; while walking or traveling, resting or walking, even when you lie down in a hospital bed.

The Rosary is the prayer of everyone — young and old. It is an easy practice, pleasing to Mary: she recommended it at Lourdes and Fatima.

The Rosary was and is constantly promoted by the Popes, and they enriched it with a Plenary Indulgence when at least a third part of it is recited.

The Rosary should be recited when we are discouraged, while fighting temptations or before making serious decisions.

The Rosary was the common practice of many Saints.

The Rosary serves for all life's needs, consoles us at the point of death. The Rosary beads will be put around our hands in the coffin. The Rosary is like a chain that will pull us up to Heaven.

How do you recite the Rosary? The simplest and most common way is to make the Sign of the Cross, enunciate the mystery, say the Our Father, ten Hail Marys, Glory, and, while saying the prayers, meditate on the episode of the mystery. The official way, when the Rosary is used as a devotional practice by a group of people or in Church, is to start with the Sign of the Cross, followed by the Apostles Creed, Our Father, three Hail Marys, Glory for an increase of faith hope and charity; then the enunciation of the mystery, Our Father, ten Hail Marys, Glory.

Let us remember that the Rosary is very pleasing to Mary, is highly efficacious to obtain graces, is the easiest way to honor God and the Blessed Virgin. The Rosary should be recited with faith, with a determined resolution to reform our lives and with devotion.

* * *

"Mary urged us to pray the Rosary, not just say it. The lip service of mumbled prayers does not please her. Mere recitation cannot bring about the vital changes in our lives that we so much need. Only devout meditation on the events in the lives of Christ and his Mother can do that," — Richard L. Rooney, S.J.

57

16: October

MEDITATIONS ON THE MYSTERIES OF THE HOLY ROSARY
(Composed and proposed by Pope John XXIII)

JOYFUL MYSTERIES (Monday and Thursday)

First Joyful Mystery: THE ANNUNCIATION
(Feast: March 25)

The Archangel Gabriel announces to the Blessed Virgin Mary the Incarnation of Our Lord Jesus Christ and her elevation to be the Mother of God. Mary accepts, declaring herself to be simply the handmaid of the Lord.

* * *

This is the first shining point of contact between heaven and earth; it is the first of those events which were to be the greatest of all time.

In this mystery the Son of God, the Word of the Father through whom "all things came into being" (Jn 1:33) in this order of creation, takes on a human nature; He becomes man in order that He might be the Redeemer and the Savior of man and of all humanity.

When Mary Immaculate, the most beautiful and most fragrant flower of all creation, said in answer to the angel's greeting: "I am the servant of the Lord" (Lk. 1:38) she accepted the honor of divine motherhood; and at that instant it was fulfilled in her. We who were once born in our father Adam as adopted children of God and who then fell from this grace are now once more brothers, adopted sons of the Father, because we have been restored to our adoption by the redemption which begins with this event. At the foot of the cross we shall all be children of Mary, with that same Jesus whom she has conceived today. From this event on she will be the Mother of God and our Mother.

What sublimity and what tenderness in this first mystery!

As we reflect on this scene, our principal and constant duty is to thank the Lord because He has deigned to come to save us and because He has become man and our human brother. He has joined us by becoming the son of a woman and by making us the adopted sons of this woman at the foot of the cross. Since we are adopted sons of His heavenly Father, He has willed that we should also be sons of the same Mother.

In the contemplation of this first scene, besides the habitual thought of gratitude, our prayer should be directed towards a real and sincere effort to acquire humility, purity, and an ardent love, for all these are virtues of which the Blessed Virgin gives us a shining example.

* * *

Holy Mary, pray for us.

58

17: October

Second Joyful Mystery: THE VISITATION

(Feast: July 2)

The Blessed Virgin Mary, moved by the virtue of charity, hastens to visit and serve her cousin Elizabeth, the expectant mother of John the Baptist.

* * *

What gentleness and charm are to be found in this three-month visit of Mary to her beloved cousin! Both of them are about to bear a child, but the motherhood of the Virgin Mary is the most sacred imaginable. A sweet harmony is to be found in the canticles that the two interchange with each other: on the one hand, "Blessed are you among women" (Lk. 1:42), and on the other, "He (the Lord) has looked upon his servant in her lowliness . . . ; all ages to come shall call me blessed" (Lk. 1:48).

The event that happens here at Ain-Karim on the hill of Hebron sheds a light, both very human and heavenly, on the bonds that unite Christian families which have been formed by the ancient school of the holy rosary: the rosary recited every evening in the intimate circle of the home; the rosary recited not just in one or a hundred or a thousand families, but by every family; the rosary recited everywhere in the world where man "suffers, struggles and prays" (A. Manzoni, *La Pentecoste,* v. 6); the rosary recited by those called by inspiration from on high to the priesthood, or to missionary work, or to a longed-for apostolate; the rosary recited by all those who are called by motives, legitimate as well as pressing, to labor, to business, to military service, to study, to teaching or to any other occupation.

During the saying of the Hail Marys of this mystery, there is a beautiful gathering of countless persons linked together by blood, by family ties, and by every bond that sanctifies and therefore strengthens the sentiments of love which bind us to those we love most: parents and children, brothers and relatives, fellow countrymen, fellow citizens. All this should be done for the purpose of sustaining, increasing, and ir-radiating that universal charity, the exercise of which is the most profound and supreme joy of our lives.

* * *

Holy Mother of God, pray for us.

59

18: October

3rd Joyful Mystery: THE BIRTH OF OUR LORD JESUS

(FEAST: December 25)

Born in the stable of Bethlehem, Jesus is laid in a manger amid utter poverty.

* * *

At the hour appointed by the laws of the human nature He has assumed, the Word of God-made-man issues from the holy tabernacle of the immaculate womb of Mary. His first appearance in the world is in a manger where animals feed and where everything is silence, poverty, simplicity, innocence. The voices of angels resound in the heavens announcing the peace which the newborn Infant brings to the world. The first worshipers are Mary, His Mother, and Joseph, His foster-father; after them, humble shepherds come from the hillside, invited by angelic voices. Later will come a caravan of distinguished persons guided from afar by a star; they will offer precious gifts pregnant with mysterious meaning.

Everything that night at Bethlehem spoke a language that the whole world could understand.

In this mystery everyone will bow in adoration before this crib. Everyone will look into the eyes of the divine Infant as they look into the distance, as if He could see all the peoples of the earth as they pass before Him, one after the other. He recognizes them all; He identifies them all, and greets them all with a smile: Jews, Romans, Greeks, Chinese, Indians, the peoples of Africa, and of every region of the universe, of every age of history. It makes no difference if the regions be far distant, solitary, remote, secret, and unexplored; nor does it matter whether the epoch is past, present, or future.

During the praying of this decade the Holy Father likes to recommend to the newborn Jesus the uncountable number of babies of all the peoples of the earth who in the preceding twenty-four hours have come to the light of day everywhere on the face of the earth. All, whether baptized or not, belong by right to Him, to this Babe born in Bethlehem. They are His brothers, called to a lordship that is the most sublime and the most gentle in the heart of man and in the history of the world. It is a lordship that alone is worthy of God and of man, a lordship of light and of peace; it is the "kingdom" we pray for in the Our Father.

* * *

Mother of Christ, pray for us.

4th Joyful Mystery: THE PRESENTATION

(FEAST: November 21)

Although not duty bound, Mary presents Jesus in the Temple and perfectly fulfills what was prescribed by the Mosaic law of purification. Simeon predicts that Jesus will be a sign of contradiction and that Mary's heart will be pierced by a sword.

* * *

Christ, carried in His mother's arms, is offered to the priest, to whom He holds out His arms: it is the meeting, the contact of the two Covenants. He is already the "revealing light to the Gentiles" (Lk. 2:32), He, the splendor of the Chosen People, the Son of Mary. Present also is Joseph who equally shares in this rite of legal offerings prescribed by the Law.

In a different but analogous way this episode is continued and perpetuated in the Church: while we recite this decade how beautiful it is to contemplate the field growing to harvest: "Open your eyes and see! The fields are shining for harvest" (Jn 4:35). This harvest consists of the joyful hopes of the priesthood and of co-workers of the priesthood; there are many of these in the kingdom of God and yet never enough. They are the youths in seminaries, in religious houses, in missionary institutes; and because all Christians are called to be apostles, they are also in Catholic universities. They are also all those other hopes of the future apostolate inseparable from the laity. It is an apostolate which grows in spite of difficulties and opposition; it enters even into nations suffering from persecution; it offers and will never cease to offer a spectacle so consoling that it calls forth words of joyful admiration.

This child is "a revealing light to the Gentiles"; the glory of the Chosen People.

"A most practical and easy way of enriching individual lives in a Christian-like manner is to imitate and follow the lessons contained in each mystery of the Rosary. . . . A prayer of love breathed from the heart; that is what Mary's Rosary must be." — Pope John XXIII.

* * *

Virgin most faithful, pray for us.

20: October
5th Joyful Mystery:THE FINDING OF JESUS IN THE TEMPLE

At the age of twelve Jesus, instead of returning to Nazareth with His parents remains in Jerusalem for three days among the doctors of the law in the Temple, listening to them and asking them questions.

* * *

Christ is now twelve years old. Mary and Joseph have brought Him with them to Jerusalem for the prescribed worship. Without warning He disappears, unseen by their vigilant and loving eyes. Their anguish is great, and for three days they search for Him in vain. Sorrow is succeeded by joy when they find Him in the area around the Temple, holding discussions with the doctors of the Law. How significant and detailed are the words with which St. Luke describes the scene: "On the third day they came upon him in the temple sitting in the midst of the teachers, listening to them and asking them questions" (Lk. 2:46). At that time a meeting such as this had a deep significance: knowledge, wisdom, guidance of practical life in the light of the Old Testament.

Such, in every age, is the task of human intelligence: to garner the wisdom of the ages, to transmit sound teaching, firmly and humbly to press ahead with scientific investigation, for we all die one after the other and we go to God, but mankind journeys toward the future.

Both on the level of supernatural and natural knowledge, Christ is never absent; He is always found there at His place: "Only one is your teacher, the Messiah" (Mt. 23:10).

This fifth decade, the last of the joyful mysteries, should be considered a specially beneficial invocation for all those who are called by God, because of their natural gifts or the circumstances of their lives, or the wishes of their superiors, to the service of truth. Whether they are engaged in research or in teaching, whether they impart knowledge long attained or new techniques, whether they write books or are concerned with audio-visual projects; all of them are called to imitate Jesus. All of these, especially journalists, since they have the particular task of honoring the truth, should communicate it with religious fidelity, with the utmost prudence, and without fantastic distortion or falsification.

Let us pray for all of them; whether they be priests or lay persons; let us pray that they may listen to the truth — and for this they need great purity of heart; that they may learn to understand the truth — and for this great humility of mind is required; that they may defend the truth — and for this they need what made the strength of Christ and of the saints: obedience. Only obedience wins peace and victory.

* * *

Mother of good counsel, pray for us.

21: October

SORROWFUL MYSTERIES (Tues. & Fri.)

1st Sorrowful Mystery: THE AGONY IN THE GARDEN

In the Garden of Gethsemane, Jesus sweats blood and prays with humility and perseverance, strengthening Himself for the Crucifixion.

* * *

The mind returns again and again to the scene of the Savior in the place and hour of His supreme abandon: "And his sweat became like drops of blood falling to the ground" (Lk. 22:24). It is an interior pain of the soul, the bitterness of an extreme loneliness, the exhaustion of a worn-out body. It is an agony that could be caused only by the passion which Jesus now sees not as distant or even as near, but as already present.

The scene of Gethsemane gives us the strength and the courage to strain our wills to accept even great suffering when that suffering is willed or permitted by God: "Not my will but yours be done" (Lk. 22:42). These are words that both wound and heal; they teach us the glowing ardor that can and should be reached by the Christian who suffers together with the suffering Christ; they give us the certainty of the indescribable merits He obtained for us, the certainty of the divine life that exists in us now through grace and will be in us later through glory.

In the present mystery the particular intention that should be considered is the "anxiety for all the churches" (2 Cor. 11-28), an anxiety that torments us, as the wind disturbed the lake of Genesaret, for the wind was against them (cf. Mt. 14:28). This is the object of the daily prayer of the Holy Father: the anxiety of the most fearful hours of his pastoral ministry; the anxiety of the Church which suffers with him throughout the world, while at the same time he suffers with the Church present and suffering in him; the anxiety of souls and whole portions of the flock of Christ who are subjected to persecution directed against the freedom to believe, to think, and to live. "Who is weak that I am not affected by it?" (2 Cor. 11:29).

This sharing in the sorrows of our brothers, this suffering with those who suffer, this weeping with those who weep (cf. Rom. 12:5) is a merciful blessing for the entire Church. Is this not what we mean by the Communion of Saints, everyone of us sharing in common the blood of Christ, the love of the saints and of good people, and also, alas! our sin and failings? We should continually reflect on this communion which is a union and, as Christ said, a kind of unity: "That they may be one" (Jn. 17:22). The cross of our Lord not only raises us up, but also draws the souls of men. "And I — once I am lifted up from the earth — will draw all men to myself" (Jn. 12:32).

* * *

Refuge of sinners, pray for us.

63

22: October

2nd Sorrowful Mystery: THE SCOURGING

Tied to a pillar, Jesus is cruelly scourged in reparation for men's many sins of impurity.

* * *

This mystery recalls to our minds the merciless lashing of the immaculate and holy body of Christ.

Human nature is composed of body and soul. The body endures humiliating temptations, while the will in its weakness can easily be carried away. In this mystery, then, there is a call to practical penance, a salutary penance, which implies and involves the true well-being of man, a well-being which comprehends bodily welfare and spiritual salvation.

The teaching that comes from this mystery is important for all. We are not called to a bloody martyrdom, but to the constant discipline and daily mortification of our passions. This road is a true way of the cross, daily, unavoidable, necessary; at times it can become heroic in its demands. By it we gradually arrive at an ever greater resemblance to Christ, at a participation in His merits, at a greater cleansing of every sin through His immaculate blood. We never arrive at this by way of easy enthusiasms or by way of useless and ineffective extravagance.

His Mother, stricken wtih sorrow, sees Him after His scourging; her affliction is overwhelming. How many mothers desire to see their children grow perfect as they initiate them into the discipline of a good training and of a sound life; yet instead they must mourn the vanishing of their hopes, saddened because so much care and anxiety have come to nothing.

The Hail Marys of this mystery, then, will ask of the Lord the gift of purity for the family, for society, and especially for young people since they are most exposed to the seduction of the senses. They will also plead for strength of character and for loyalty at all costs to the teachings they have received and the resolutions they have made.

* * *

Mother most chaste, pray for us.

23: October
3rd Sorrowful Mystery: THE CROWNING WITH THORNS

Jesus is crowned with thorns and mocked in atonement for many evil thoughts, desires and sentiments.

* * *

The contemplation of this mystery is especially concerned with those who bear the burdensome responsibility of the direction of social life: it is the mystery of those who govern, who make laws, and who judge. On the head of this King, there is a crown of thorns. They too wear crowns, which have their own undeniable dignity and distinction; they are crowns representing an authority that comes from God and is therefore divine. Yet interwoven into this crown are things that press down, that pierce, that bring perplexity, that tempt to bitterness; it is in brief a crown of thorns and of worry; and it is this even aside from the sorrow caused by the misfortunes and sins of men, which is a sorrow all the more keen as one loves them and has the duty of representing to them the Father who is in heaven.

Another useful application of the mystery would be to consider the serious responsibilities of those who have received greater talents and therefore are bound to bring forth fruit in proportionate measure through the continual exercise of their faculties and of their intelligence. The ministry of the mind, that is the duty of those who are more endowed to act as a light and a guide to others, should be carried out patiently, resisting all the temptations of pride, of selfishness, and of disintegration which is destructive.

"O blessed Rosary of Mary, how sweetly consoling it is to see you held in the hands of innocent persons, of holy priests, of pure souls, of young and old, of so many who appreciate the value and efficacy of prayer, held by countless and pious throngs as an emblem and a banner of good omen of peace in the heart of men of peace for all mankind! . . . Oh! how beautiful is the Rosary of the innocent child and of those who are sick, of the consecrated virgin in the seclusion of the cloister or in the humble and self-sacrificing apostolate of charity; of the man and woman, father and mother of a family, imbued with an exalted sense of noble and Christian responsibility; of humble families faithful to the ancient tradition of the home! . . . Mary's Rosary is thus raised to the height of a great public and universal prayer for all the ordinary and extraordinary needs of Holy Church, of nations and of the entire world." — Pope John XXIII in *Il Religioso Convegno*, Sept. 29, 1961.

* * *

Mother most pure, pray for us.

65

3

24: October

4th Sorrowful Mystery: THE CARRYING OF THE CROSS

Unjustly condemned to death by Pontius Pilate, Jesus carries the heavy cross to Calvary.

* * *

Human life is a continual, long and burdensome pilgrimage; it is an upward journey over the rocky ascents that are marked to be the lot of all men. In the present mystery Christ represents the human race. If each man did not possess his own cross, sooner or later he would fall by the wayside, tempted by selfishness or by indifference.

By contemplating Christ as He climbs up Calvary, we learn — more through the heart than the mind — to embrace and to kiss the cross, to carry it with generosity and even with joy, as we read in the *Imitation of Christ*: "In the cross lies our salvation, our life; in the cross we have a defense against our foes. In the cross we have a pouring-in of heavenly sweetness" (Bk. II, chap. 12:2).

And should not our prayer extend also to Mary, who in her sorrow follows Christ in a spirit of intimate participation in His merits and in His sorrows?

This mystery should set before our eyes the vast vision of those in tribulation: orphans, the aged, the sick, prisoners, the weak, and refugees. For all of these let us ask for strength and the consolation that only hope can give.

Let us repeat tenderly and with the hidden interior tears of the soul: "Hail, O cross, our only hope" (Vesper hymn of Passion Sunday).

———

"May the Rosary be ever in your hands; may the Marian prayer continue to sanctify your family reunion every night, and may it give the spiritual tone to your whole life." — Pope John XXIII, Sept. 11, 1960.

* * *

Comforter of the afflicted, pray for us.

25: October

5th Sorrowful Mystery: THE CRUCIFIXION

Jesus is crucified, suffers for three hours and dies to save us from eternal damnation.

* * *

"Life and death meet in a wonderful battle" (Sequence of the Easter Mass); life and death are the two significant and decisive elements of the sacrifice of Christ. From Bethlehem's smile — one such as is found in all the sons of men at their first appearance on this earth — to Calvary's last breath and gasp which gather into one all our sorrows in order to hallow them and which expiate our sins in order to blot them out; this is the life of Christ on earth among us. And Mary stands near the cross as she once stood beside the Babe of Bethlehem. Let us pray to her, our Mother, that she may pray for us "now and at the hour of our death."

In this mystery we see outlined the mystery of those who will never acknowledge the blood which has been poured forth for them by the Son of God. It is the mystery especially of obstinate sinners, of unbelievers, of those who receive and then reject the light of the gospel. Such thoughts cause prayer to break forth in one immense sigh, in one burst of heartfelt reparation in a worldwide view of the apostolate. We beg wholeheartedly that the precious blood poured out for all men may at long last bring salvation and conversion to all men and that the blood of Christ may be to all the pledge and promise of life eternal.

———

"The power of the Rosary is beyond description . . . The Rosary is the easiest prayer to say . . . All the idle moments of one's life can be sanctified, thanks to the Rosary. As we walk the streets, we pray with the rosary well hidden in our hand or in our pocket; driving an automobile, the little knobs under most steering wheels can serve as counters for the decades. While waiting to be served at a lunchroom, or waiting for a train, or in a store; or while playing dummy at bridge; or when conversation or a lecture lags — all these moments can be sanctified and made to serve inner peace, thanks to a prayer that enables one to pray at all times and under all circumstances. If you wish to convert anyone to the fullness of the knowledge of Our Lord and of His Mystical Body, then teach him the Rosary. One of two things will happen. Either he will stop saying the Rosary — or he will get the gift of faith." — Bishop Fulton Sheen.

* * *

Mother of Our Redeemer, pray for us.

GLORIOUS MYSTERIES (Wed., Sat., and Sun.)

1st Glorious Mystery: THE RESURRECTION
(FEAST: Easter)

Jesus Christ rises gloriously from the sepulcher.

* * *

This is the mystery of death challenged and defeated. The resurrection marks the definitive triumph of Christ and it is at the same time the assurance of the triumph of the Catholic Church over adversities and persecutions past and present. "Christ conquers, reigns and rules." We do well to recall that the first appearance of the risen Christ was to the pious women who had been close to Him during his humble life and who remained close to Him even on Calvary.

In the splendor of this mystery the gaze of our faith goes out to the living souls now united with the risen Christ, the souls of those dearest to us, the souls of those who lived with us and whose sufferings we shared. In the light of the resurrection of Christ there rises up in our hearts the remembrance of the dead. We remember and pray for them in the very sacrifice of our crucified and risen Lord, and they still share the best part of our life which is prayer and Jesus.

It is not without reason that the Eastern liturgy concludes the funeral rite with an Alleluia for all the dead. Let us ask for the dead the light of an eternal resting place, while at the same time our thoughts are directed to the resurrection of our own mortal remains: "I await the resurrection of the dead." Learning to wait, trusting always in the precious promise of which the resurrection of Christ is a sure pledge — this is a foretaste of heaven.

"Carry the Rosary with you every day of your life, during your generous adolescence, your ardent youth, and in your mature and working years." — Pope John XXIII, March 4, 1963.

* * *

Cause of our joy, pray for us.

2nd Glorious Mystery: THE ASCENSION

(FEAST: Thursday, 40 days after Easter)

On Mt. Olivet, Our Savior showed Himself to the apostles, to Mary and to one hundred twenty people. After blessing them, He triumphantly ascended into heaven.

* * *

In this scene let us contemplate the consummation and final fulfillment of the promises of Christ. It is His response to our longing for paradise. His final return to the Father, from whom He had descended among us in this world, is a surety for us all, to whom He has promised and prepared a place above: "I am indeed going to prepare a place for you" (Jn. 14:2).

This mystery, above all others, is a light and a guide for those souls who strive to follow their proper vocations. We see within it that spiritual longing, that yearning to soar upwards which burns in the hearts of priests who are not held down and distracted by the goods of this earth but seek only to open to themselves and to others the ways that lead to sanctity and perfection. This is that level of grace to which one and all must come; priests, religious, missionaries, lay people devoted to God and the Church, souls that are "the aroma of Christ" (2 Cor. 2:15). Where such are, Christ is felt to be near; and they already live in a continual union with the life of heaven.

This mystery teaches and urges us not to allow ourselves to be hampered by things that burden and weigh us down, but to abandon ourselves to the will of the Lord who draws us heavenward. As Jesus ascends into heaven to return to His Father, His arms are open to bless the apostles and all those who follow them in their belief in Him. In the hearts of such there is a calm and serene assurance of a final reunion with Him and with all the redeemed, in everlasting bliss.

"We want to declare in complete frankness and simplicity that the years have made Mary's Rosary all the dearer to Us. We never fail to recite it each day in its entirety and We intend to recite it with particular devotion during the month of October." — Pope John XXIII, Sept. 26, 1959.

* * *

Gate of Heaven, pray for us.

69

28: October

3rd Glorious Mystery: THE COMING OF THE HOLY SPIRIT

(FEAST: Pentecost Sunday)

The Holy Spirit descends upon Mary and the Apostles to enlighten, comfort and sanctify them.

* * *

At the Last Supper the apostles received the promise of the Spirit; later in the Cenacle, with Christ gone but Mary present, they receive Him as Christ's supreme gift. Indeed, what is His Spirit if not the Consoler and Giver of Life to men? The Holy Spirit continues to pour forth His grace on and in the Church day by day; all ages and all men belong to the Spirit and to the Church. The Church's triumphs are not always externally visible, but they are always there, full of surprises and marvels.

The Hail Marys of this mystery are directed towards a special intention in this year of enthusiasm as we see the pilgrim Church plan and prepare for the Ecumenical Council. The Council is to be a new Pentecost of faith, of the apostolate, and of extraordinary graces for the well-being of men and the peace of the entire world. Mary, the Mother of Christ and our own sweet Mother, was with the apostles in the Cenacle at Pentecost. Let us ever remain close to her through the rosary during this year. Our prayers, united with hers, will effect once more the ancient event of Pentecost; it will be like the rising of a new day, the dawn of new activity for the Church as she grows holier and more catholic in these modern days.

———

"It is a pleasure to recall that Our predecessor (Pius XII) urged all the faithful to the pious recitation of the Rosary during October in the Encyclical Ingruentium malorum. *We would like to repeat one admonition from that Encyclical: 'Fly with greater confidence to the Mother of God. She has always been the first refuge of the Christian people in the hour of danger, because 'She has been made the cause of salvation for the whole human race.' "* — Pope John XXIII, Sept. 26, 1959.

* * *

Queen of the Apostles, pray for us.

4th Glorious Mystery: THE ASSUMPTION OF MARY

(FEAST: August 15)

Her mission accomplished on earth, Mary is assumed into heaven, body and soul, with marvelous glory.

* * *

The lovely image of Mary becomes glowing and brilliant in this greatest of exaltations that a creature may have. How full of grace, of sweetness, and of solemnity is the dormition of Mary, as the Christians of the East love to think about it. She lies there in the serene sleep of death. Jesus stands beside her, and clasps her soul, as if it were a tiny child, to His heart, to indicate the miracle of Mary's immediate resurrection and glorification.

The Christians of the West, on the other hand, prefer to raise their eyes and their hearts to follow Mary as she is assumed body and soul into the eternal kingdom. It is in this way that our greatest artists have represented her in her incomparable beauty. Let us, too, go with her, borne aloft by her escort of angels!

On days of sorrow this scene is a source of consolation and fidelity for those privileged souls — and we can all be such if we respond to grace — whom God is silently preparing for the greatest of triumphs, that of sainthood.

The mystery of the Assumption brings home to us the thought of death, including our own; it gives us a sense of serene abandon of ourselves, for it makes us understand and welcome the thought that the Lord will be near us, as we should wish Him to be, in our last agony, to gather into His hands our immortal souls.

May your favor be always with us, O Immaculate Virgin!

———

"Individuals, whatever their spiritual status may be, will undoubtedly find in the fervent recitation of the Holy Rosary, an invitation to regulate their lives in conformity with Christian principles. They will, in truth, find the Rosary a spring of most abundant graces to help them in fulfilling faithfully their duties in life." — Pope John XXIII, May 1, 1959.

* * *

Queen assumed into heaven, pray for us.

30: October

5th Glorious Mystery: THE CROWNING OF OUR LADY

(FEAST: Queenship of Mary, August 22)

Mary is crowned Queen of heaven and earth, dispenser of all graces and our most loving mother.

* * *

The meaning of the entire rosary is summed up in this scene of joy and glory, with which it ends.

The great theme that opened with the Annunciation of the angel to Mary has passed like a stream of fire and light through each of the mysteries: God's eternal plan for our salvation. It has been imaged to us in one scene after another; it has been present in all the mysteries up to now; and now it ends with God in the splendor of heaven.

The glory of Mary, the Mother of Christ and our Mother, shines in the splendor of the most august Trinity and is dazzlingly reflected in the Church in all her states: triumphant in heaven, suffering patiently in purgatory in the confident expectation of heaven, and militant on earth.

O Mary, pray with us, pray for us, as we know and feel you do. How real are the delights, how lofty the glory in the divine-human interchange of sentiments, words and actions, which the rosary has given and continues to give to us. It softens our human afflictions; it is a foretaste of the peace of the other world; it is our hope of eternal life.

PRAYING THE ROSARY TOGETHER

Saying the Rosary by yourself is fine, but wouldn't it be wonderful if others joined you? If you so desire, become a member of one of the following Rosary Associations:

1) THE CONFRATERNITY OF THE ROSARY
2) CONFRATERNITY OF THE HOLY ROSARY
3) THE PERPETUAL ROSARY
4) THE LIVING ROSARY
5) THE FAMILY ROSARY CRUSADE

* * *

Queen of all Angels and Saints, pray for us.

31: October

THE PROMISES OF MARY, QUEEN OF THE HOLY ROSARY

(Attributed to St. Dominic and taken from the writings of Blessed Alan)

Keep a blessed rosary with you day and night. Mary will protect you always.

* * *

1. Whoever will faithfully serve me by the recitation of the Rosary shall receive signal graces.

2. To all who recite my Rosary devoutly, I promise my special protection and very great graces.

3. The Rosary will be a very powerful armor against hell. It will destroy vice, deliver from sin, and dispel heresy.

4. The Rosary will make virtue and good works flourish, and will obtain for souls the most abundant divine mercies; it will substitute in hearts love of God for love of the world, elevate them to desire heavenly and eternal goods. Oh, that souls would sanctify themselves by this means!

5. Those who entrust themselves to me through the Rosary will not perish.

6. Those who shall recite my Rosary piously, considering its mysteries, will not be overwhelmed by misfortune, nor die a bad death. The sinner will be converted, the just will grow in grace and become worthy of eternal life.

7. Whoever will have a true devotion for the Rosary shall not die without the Sacraments of the Church.

8. Those who faithfully recite the Rosary shall have during their life and at their death the light of God and the plenitude of His graces; at the moment of death they shall participate in the merits of the saints in paradise.

9. I will deliver very promptly from purgatory the souls devoted to my Rosary.

10. The true children of my Rosary will enjoy great glory in heaven.

11. What you shall ask through the Rosary you shall obtain.

12. Those who propagate my Rosary will obtain through me aid in all their necessities.

13. I have obtained from my Son that all members of the Rosary Confraternity shall have the saints of heaven for their intercessors in life and in death.

14. Those who recite my Rosary faithfully are all my beloved children, the brothers and sisters of Jesus Christ.

15. Devotion to my Rosary is a special sign of predestination.

* * *

Queen of the Holy Rosary, pray for us.

73

IN PRAISE OF THE VIRGIN MARY, OUR SWEET MOTHER
By the Servant of God, Rev. James Alberione, S.S.P.
Founder of the Pauline Religious Congregations

"O Mary, it is sweet to turn my first look upon you in the morning, to walk beneath your mantle during the day, or fall asleep under your gaze at night.

"Through the grace of Baptism Mary introduced us to the Christian life; through the grace of the Sacraments she introduced us to a life of sanctity; with the grace of final perseverance she will introduce us to eternal life.

"Let us entrust our temporal and spiritual needs to Mary. If our necessities are great, Mary's power is also great; and if we ask with faith, we shall certainly receive.

"Mary had a unique twofold mission: that of giving the physical Jesus Christ to the world, and that of forming the mystical Christ which is the Church. As she is Mother of Jesus Christ, so she is the Mother of the Church. And as she held the Church in her arms, it was the same care for Jesus Christ extended now to all the Church. A mission on earth and a mission in heaven. Oh, what a part Mary has in the history of each soul, and what a part in the history of the Church!

"Discouraged souls: turn to Mary! You sinners who feel your humiliation, turn to Mary! In doubts, in temptations, in daily encountered difficulties, in times of distrust, turn to Mary! Always to Mary. Call on Mary in every situation and refer to her in the way that a needy child looks to its mother and is sure of finding a Mother thinking of its concerns.

"We present ourselves to Mary so as to be more of Jesus. What do we present? First, our internal faculties: the soul with its intelligence and will, all its strength. We offer our bodies and all of our senses: eyes, tongue and touch. We give of our good works, merits and virtues: everything that is possible to give to Mary. We offer the merits of our past life so that they may be preserved and one day glorified. We donate whatever we may be doing and all of our current resolutions.

"The world must return to Jesus Christ through Mary. The world must refer to the Church, to Jesus Christ, to His Vicar — through Mary. When devotion to Mary is a deep part of a soul, and when devotion to Mary becomes a part of the world, then there will be a transformation — a transformation that is spiritual, intellectual and a life-force.

"Mary is like a mould. We must place our souls in Mary's hands and let her give it form. She will shape it with the same simplicity, silence and humility which characterized her own comportment."

75

IN PAISE OF MARY, MOTHER OF GOD and OUR MOTHER

"We praise Mary's virginity, we admire her humility; but because we are poor sinners mercy attracts us more and tastes sweeter; we embrace mercy more lovingly, we remember it oftener, and invoke it more earnestly." — St. Bernard.

"Jesus and Mary, my most sweet loves, for you may I suffer, for you may I die; grant that I may be in all things yours and in nothing mine." — St. Alphonsus Rodriquez.

"If all the stars were tongues and all the grains of sand were words, they still would not be able to say all the glories bestowed on Mary's soul by God." — St. Thomas of Villanova.

"Mary is the Mother of the Mystical Body and as such, she never condemns or disrupts it, but reanimates it and vivifies all who are presented to her." — Bossuet.

"Place yourself in her hands and repeat often to her: Into your hands, O Lady, I commend my spirit." — St. Gabriel of the Sorrowful Mother.

"Hail, O most brilliant star, font of eternal light; open the doors of glory to us. Amen. — St. Jerome.

"The thoughts of Mary brings joy to the afflicted, fervor to the weak, and calls the wayward back to the path of salvation." — Landolfo of Sassonia.

"How admirable is the name of Mary! He who repeats it often will not be afraid at the point of death." — St. Bonaventure.

"After God, it is impossible to think of anything greater than His Mother." — St. Anselm of Aosta.

"O my Mother Mary, I want to love you with my whole heart!" — St. John Neumann.

"I am the Lady of the Rosary." — "I shall come to ask for the consecration of Russia to my Immaculate Heart, and the Communion of Reparation of the First Saturdays. If my requests are heeded, Russia will be converted, and there will be peace . . ."

"In the end, my Immaculate Heart will triumph . . . and a period of peace will be granted to the world." — Words of Our Lady of Fatima, 13th of July of 1917.

OTHER PUBLICATIONS ON MARIOLOGY — Alba House

MARY: Mother of Christ and of Christians
by: Rev. Joseph-Marie Perrin, O.P.

"Fr. Perrin manages to bring a great deal of originality into the mainstream of Mariology. It is undoubtedly due to his years of meditation on the Blessed Mother. Noteworthy is his use of quotations from the various Marian saints. Parish libraries should want a copy of this book. Priests who need homily material on the Blessed Virgin will find this book an ample treasury of Marian ideas." THE PRIEST $3.50 — paper

* * *

THE IMAGE OF MARY: According To The Evangelists
by: Rev. Horacio Bojorge, S.J.

"This book on the image of Mary seen by each evangelist serves at least two purposes. First the reader gains valuable insight into the person and role of Mary. Second, this very process also affords the reader the opportunity to identify some of the significant differences among the evangelists. This work is to be highly recommended for adult religious education classes, personal enrichment, and personal prayer." — PASTORAL LIFE $2.75 — paper

* * *

THE ROSARY: A Gospel Prayer
by: W. J. Harrington, O.P.

The author sets out to study the firm Gospel foundation of the Rosary. He does not intend to update the prayer or suggest a new way of saying it but carefully examines its New Testament grounding with the eye of a Scripture expert. $2.95 — paper

Appendix

GREATEST ARTISTS' TRIBUTE TO THE BEAUTY OF MARY

MAGNIFICAT   Sandro Botticelli

THE ESPOUSAL OF MARY   Raffaello Sanzio

OUR LADY OF THE VEIL   Carlo Dolci

81

THE ADORATION   Filippo Lippi

OUR LADY OF THE CHAIR   Raffaello Sanzio

OUR LADY OF THE GOLD FINCH   Raffaello Sanzio

HEAD OF THE VIRGIN   Filippo Lippi

85

HEAD OF THE VIRGIN   Ghirlandaio

86

THE VIRGIN WITH SON   Murillo

HEAD OF THE VIRGIN   Filippo Lippi

HOLY FAMILY   Botticelli

HEAD OF THE VIRGIN   B. Luini

90

THE VIRGIN OF THE CLUSTER OF GRAPES   Pierre Mignard

HEAD OF THE VIRGIN   Perugino

92

ASSUMPTION   Tiziano

OUR LADY OF THE POMEGRANATE   Sandro Botticelli